Sheba's Song

J.A.HARBISON

EDITED BY
DEEPIKA DAVIDAR

Hal, Sheila, Anna, Rachel
The Bestest of
friends !
Joe

Sheba's Song
The Story of an Indian Girl and Her American Sponsor

Copyright © 2002 by J.A. Harbison
ALL RIGHTS RESERVED

ISBN 0-9727279-0-6

Published by :
WorldChristian News & Books
PO Box 26479
Colorado Springs, CO 80936
USA

Packaged by Pine Hill Graphics

Cover Design & Layout : Shini & Rob Abraham

Cover Photo : Create International

Printed in the United States of America
For Worldwide Distribution

For additional copies of Sheba's Song, please contact the publisher:
WorldChristian News & Books
PO Box 26479
Colorado Springs, CO 80936
USA

1-888-WCN.NEWS (926-6397)
wcnnews@aol.com
Online Bookstore: www.ywam.org/books/

Sheba's Song

J.A.HARBISON

EDITED BY
DEEPIKA DAVIDAR

WORLDCHRISTIAN BOOKS

For Colleen

Acknowledgements

Sheba's Song grew from a chance meeting in a congested slum north of Chennai. I went there to meet with a sponsored child, a random selection from among thousands. But I was drawn to a quiet girl of nineteen whose eyes had caught mine in the courtyard of her small home. I interviewed most of the members of her family but was impressed by this young lady, the second eldest of the offspring, who was determined to tell her story. We sat in a crowded living room, weighed upon by the monsoon humidity and Sheba began to pour forth her tale while mother and grandmother nodded approvingly. Although the story of Sheba is fictionalized, the essence is not. The joy and pathos described is an everyday reality for millions of children and their families in India.

I would like to acknowledge the following people, without whom the telling of this story would not have been possible: Mathew George, VBL Raju and all in the Compassion India Office for making my visits to Maduma Nagar possible and for introducing me to Sheba and her family. Victor and Kerryn Selvaraj, thanks for the use of your veranda, sweet memories of your beautiful children, and the thrill of riding in your Fiat, (the oldest car in India). Helen and Thomas Prabhakaran, thanks for fine food, wise counsel and warm friendship. Giggles Bookstore, for your literary counsel, it has provided me with hours of enjoyment in research and reading. Wess Stafford, Larry Yonker and Devlin Donaldson for inspiration and friendship and Steve Wamberg, Clint McCowen and Emma Garrow for your comments on the original manuscript and Regina Hopewell for not allowing me to give up. Special acknowledgment is given to my editor, Deepika Davidar, who not only helped to make this a very readable story but an enjoyable experience.

And to Sheba, thank you for sharing not only your pain but also the joy of healing with me.

J.A.Harbison

"…And believe me, from experience of children, I know that they have perhaps a finer sense of honor than you or I have. The greatest lessons of life, if we would but stoop and humble ourselves, we would learn not from the grown up learned men, but from the so-called ignorant children. If we are to reach real peace in this world, and if we are to carry on a real war against war, we shall have to begin with children; and if they will grow up in their natural innocence, we won't have to struggle, we won't have to pass fruitless idle resolutions, but we shall go from love to love and peace to peace…"

Mahatma Gandhi

Prologue

September 3, 1999

Mr. Daniel Marshall,
Editor,
Harder and Struell Publishers,
Newport Beach, California.

Dear Dan,

Greetings, old friend! You may know that last October I had the opportunity to travel to India again. Hard to believe it's been nearly fifteen years since you and I made our way from Madras to Patna by buses, trains, and those wonderful local cars that look like inflated Volkswagens. Little and much has changed in India since our adventures there. For one thing, Madras is no longer Madras; it's been renamed 'Chennai'. Sounds more like the original name, I think.

As I said then, I say today - a person does not go to India and return unchanged. It's an amazing country. I only wish you could have been with me, Dan. We could have reminisced over our days of being 'barefoot developers' in India twenty years ago!

I went to India to do a program evaluation for a large child development agency. They had heard about my work and knew me to be a Tamil speaker (well, I was one anyway!). I was thrilled to be back among familiar people and food. While in Madras, I had the opportunity to spend quality time with some of the organization's staff and visit a number of their projects. I have to tell you, Dan, this trip made a believer out of me.

I doubt you've forgotten how our old mentor, Reverend Jessup, used to ridicule sponsorship programs. Remember his sarcastic remark about sponsorship? 'Feed the children and buy their souls.'

I loved our old mentor but I have to say that had he dug into what these programs do, he may have been more sympathetic.

I believe I can hear you saying, "Stan has traded sound development for an easy fix remedy." But hear me out, Dan. On second thought, don't hear me out, hear Sheba out. Sheba is a young woman I met at one of the projects. As you can imagine, I went to Chennai a skeptic, prepared to really test the organization and find out what made it tick. I suspected I would find a few rich cats skimming the cream off the projects.

While at a project in a suburb called Perambur, I was about to start the old routine. You know, checking out the books, child records and financial ledger, asking sixty-four questions, and ending up confused. Instead, I asked the project manager, a sharp man named Valar, if I could speak with a formerly sponsored child. What I really wanted to know was: Did it matter? Did all the sponsorship, letters and programs really make a difference in the lives of these kids?

. Valar checked his files and pointed to a name, 'Dorairaj'. Skeptical soul that I am, I ignored his suggestion and pointed to a name at the beginning of the list, 'Sunderraj'.

"Is this family still here?" I asked.

"Yes, yes!" replied Valar in a voice that sounded like a violin pitched an octave too high. "No problem. Lives nearby. Come I will show you."

We sped off in Valar's old Fiat that, I am not kidding you, looked as though Marco Polo might have ridden in. I could actually see the ground flying by through the rust-eaten floorboard. Valar quickly (too quickly me thinks!) made the two-kilometer drive to a locality in Perambur called Maduma Nagar. We wove our way through a dirty neighborhood. It consisted of an assortment of clay houses and squalid tenement buildings punctuated by shrines, temples, and sidewalk markets overflowing with fruits and vegetables.

When Valar brought the car to a halt in a cloud of dust we found ourselves outside a little house. It was a squarish house, faded green and connected to a crooked group of row houses that followed a canal. I thought we would quickly be surrounded by a bunch of noisy, excited kids. But all that greeted us was the sight of an old lady silently weaving a basket. She was seated on a small stool in the dark doorway of her house.

"My evaluation efforts are heading down a dead-end street here," I thought with a shrug. I was about to turn and leave when the old lady looked up at us. She smiled. And I forgot about leaving. Her gaunt face and broad, gentle smile filled me with a sense of pity and curiosity.

Now Dan, I hope you're still reading this. I know you get a lot of these queries, but remember I am no author; I'm a friend so you owe this to me. (Dan, are you still there?)

Valar introduced me to the old lady and I stumbled along in my now wretched Tamil (you would have laughed out loud!). And that's when Sheba, the woman's daughter, came out. The radiance of her smile is with me as I write this. Sheba happened to be visiting her mother and on hearing my botched attempts at Tamil, came out and asked, in perfect English, if I would like some tea.

To tell you more would spoil the story. I can only say that over the next two days I spent time with Sheba and her family and heard firsthand what sponsorship had meant to her life and, more, what she did with her opportunities.

Now here's the kicker. You know that sponsored children are required to write to their sponsors. The aim is to build a relationship between sponsor and child. It seems that Sheba got quite a few letters from her sponsor, a couple named Crenshaw from Crofton, Iowa. Like most children, Sheba found it difficult to express herself in writing so, in her replies, she said pretty much what most kids would say, that is, as little as possible. Recently however, on rereading her sponsor's letters, which she had kept carefully all these years, she decided to write detailed replies to his letters. Mind you, it had been over ten years since she had heard from him.

What she eventually wrote was more than a letter. It is this manuscript accompanying my letter to you. Sheba asked if I would carry the manuscript back to the States and look up Mr. Crenshaw. I agreed and took the manuscript with me after I'd finished my evaluation of the South India Sponsorship Program. (By the way, I gave them a pretty good overall rating).

When I got back, I made a few calls to Crofton, Iowa to confirm the address. That's when the bottom fell out of my briefcase. I called the Crenshaw house and a man named Randy answered. When I asked for Clayton Crenshaw, he replied that that was his father who had passed away two summers ago! I explained the situation and Randy said that he would like to take a look at those letters.

Randy read the letters and called me a month later. He said the letters were in the mail again. He said that since it was I that brought them back from India, it was I who should make sure they "got read". (I love the way country folk think!)

Randy and his wife are also sponsors of four children. He said this was a result of his parents' awesome experience with Sheba. Seems the whole family is excited about sponsorship, even the kids are sending cards and letters. Randy suggested that I take a look at the letters and see what I thought.

Well, my old friend, what I think is that these ought to be published. I don't want to tell you how to do your job, (I know you wouldn't allow it anyway) but I wonder if there is something here that others ought to hear about as well.

Over to you my friend! Let me know what you think.

Warm regards from a friend who remembers you young and skinny,

Stan Housman

Clayton and Sue Ellen Crenshaw
63 Ash Street
Crofton, Iowa

October 18, 1978

Dear Sheba,

Greetings from the United States of America! I doubt you have ever heard of me, but I am writing to introduce myself to you and your family. You see, my wife and I have been invited to sponsor a child like you somewhere in the world. I chose India since I have always wanted to travel there. Unfortunately, I've never had the opportunity. Our names are Clayton and Sue Ellen Crenshaw. You may call me Clay. Most children around here call Mrs. Crenshaw, Auntie Sue Ellen.

I have a picture of you lying here on my writing desk. It shows a pretty girl, standing straight as an arrow, with her hands to her side. In fact, Sheba, it looks like you are a little afraid. Do you have your picture taken often? I can see that you have on a dark dress that looks to me like a school uniform. Your hair is in two ponytails tied with small pieces of light-colored ribbon. It looks like you are standing in front of a hedge or some bushes. On your shoulder is the large, dark hand of an unseen person. I think it must be a man, I can see the cuff of a white long-sleeved shirt. Perhaps he was trying to assure you that having your picture

11

taken wouldn't hurt! I am smiling as I write this.

Behind those serious brown eyes of yours I can see that you are a very smart girl. You certainly don't look poor. You look like a person who will get what she wants, even if it means working hard for it.

And that is all I know about you. Wait a minute. I see that I do have some information about you after all. Along with the picture, I have a short letter that tells me a little more about you. You are Sheba Victoria. You were born on August 21st, 1970, and live in Maduma Nagar, a locality in Perambur, which is a suburb of Madras. I also read that you are learning English and that we may write to each other in English, which is lucky for me, as I know nothing of the Indian language.

Well, Sheba, perhaps I should do as much for you, then we can start off with the same amount of information about each other. You already know my name. I was born on March 15, 1918. My wife, Sue Ellen, was born two years after me on July 10. My wife and I were both born in Iowa, the Midwest part of the USA. It's a large farming and dairy State. Sheba, some-day I'll tell you about Iowa and what it's like here. I'm sending you a picture of my family. It's a few years old but you'll get an idea of what we all look like. Their names are on the back of the picture. I was born into a farming family and until a few years ago I was a farmer. Now I'm a carpenter. Apart from a weak back and Auntie Sue Ellen's stiffness in her legs, we are in good health.

Sheba, I hope to get to learn more about you and want you to know that Auntie and I will be praying for you each day around the breakfast table. That's our custom and it's the time when we pray for our family and friends.

Well Sheba, I have said a lot already and will close for now. Tell me, Sheba, what's it like growing up in Madras?

With Love,

Clay and Auntie Sue Ellen

Dear Mr. Crenshaw,

As a little girl, I never thought of myself as poor. It seemed to me as though we were quite well off because my earliest memories are happy ones. Our home was small and consisted of two rooms, a living room that served as a bedroom by night and a small windowless kitchen where my mother spent much of her time. Cramped as it appears today, it seemed spacious in the eyes of a child.

Our home was one of four living units, linked together like a giant green caterpillar winding along the narrow banks of the Koobar canal.

Appa and Amma often talked long into the night, discussing the lives of relatives and friends, some long since dead. They must have thought I was fast asleep. On the contrary, I was soaking in the precious tales told in the darkness. These stories were woven together to form the tapestry of my family's history.

Ours is a story-telling society, Mr. Crenshaw. Epic poems and colorful mythologies are plentiful. While your history and legends are documented by the variety of media you have in your country, our history is inscribed upon the hearts and tender minds of each new generation. Those long-ago stories remain with me and give meaning to a humble life such as mine.

My grandmother often told me that each person has been blessed with a special *talandhu* or gift. The secret of life is to discover your gift and use it to serve your community. I learned early that I have two gifts. I am a listener, and I love to tell stories. Some say I talk too much and I confess it often got me into trouble in my school years. My skills at listening and story telling were honed within my family and at school. And, in my own family, I continue to weave together the stories of our lives.

Now, as an adult, I can reflect on my youth. The innocent hopes and dreams of a poor child; finishing school; having a suitable husband chosen for me; and raising a family of my own. But the fulfillment of those dreams didn't come without a struggle.

In part, it was your sponsorship that brought me to the threshold of hope and lifted me to the dizzy heights of possibilities. Yet, it was at those heights that I feared failure. I feared crossing

13

the threshold that marked my personal divide between hope and despair. I confess. I nearly turned back more than once.

Dear Mr. Crenshaw, I now know that you are not the god-like sponsor of my childish imagination. You are a good, honest, and hardworking man. As I reread your letters, I see that you are a farmer and a carpenter. Reading between the lines (as I am able to do at the age of almost thirty), I understand that you take pride in what you do. Once you told me about a special project you undertook that involved building some bleachers for a small baseball park. You explained in more detail than a twelve-year-old girl, who had never heard of baseball, could take in. You mentioned the required seating capacity, the necessary strength of the structure and so forth. Now I look at those pages and read...

"After Earl Thornton and I finished work on the bleachers, I just stood there and watched the kids play and felt like I was a youngster again."

In another letter, you sent me a picture of you and Auntie Sue Ellen standing in the garden of a simple white wooden house surrounded by a small fence. I was surprised to see that picture. You looked rather old and gray and your wife standing next to you, looked very thin in her dark slacks. You wore a baseball cap that concealed, I suspect, a baldhead and more years than I thought could belong to you.

Even though I understood your questions without translation (thanks to your sponsorship I was able to attend an English medium school), I was at a loss to answer you in the way you may have wished.

For instance, a special trait of your letter writing was to almost always end your letters with a question. Your questions were touching and thoughtful but to a child who found it difficult to reply in detail, bewildering. At the time, I thought it a quirk of an old man. I now see the wisdom in your questions. I have borrowed your technique and make it a habit to ask my students the same kind of questions. Questions designed to probe and provoke my students into thinking.

I've been a teacher for nearly ten years in a public school. Our classes are packed, sometimes with ninety squirming adolescents, and it is not always possible to give individual attention. Even so, I

14

search out those children with a spark of curiosity and a hunger for learning. Through writing assignments based on the very questions you asked me, I encourage children to learn by being observant.

Mr. Crenshaw, I am writing this 'letter' to repay you in my own way by sharing some of my life with you, even as you shared a measure of hope and practical assistance with a poor girl whom, I trust you will agree, turned out all right. I have picked out a few of your letters and chosen to answer those questions that will give you an insight into my growing years.

This, then, is my story. The story of Sheba Victoria, first child of Mohan and Victoria Sunderraj and granddaughter of Albert and Aruna Sunderraj.

I mourn not for the past;
indeed,
I only remember the benefits
That have been done on my behalf.

Indian Proverb

It's difficult to believe that more than twenty years have passed since I received your first letter. I remember the excitement of that day though I had little understanding of what sponsorship meant or would do for my family and me. I do remember spinning around in dizzy circles when my brother Baskar gave me the big news.

"You have a sponsor!" he shouted when I arrived home from school. I was eight years old and in Standard Three.

"I have a sponsor?" I asked incredulously.

In my childish ignorance I thought I must be someone very special. I remember the sensation of well being caused by knowing that somewhere in a far-off land was a person who cared for me.

The prospect of sponsorship brought images of untold opportunity. It meant cash for tuition and that made the difference between an education and none. I had sometimes heard Amma and Appa speaking softly as they discussed the education of their children. They debated which of us showed the most potential, and calculated how much money it would cost to get one or more through school. All poor families hope to see at least one or more of their children complete secondary school and if possible get a college education. Our family was no exception. An education would mean tremendous opportunities, especially when compared to the prospects of an uneducated laborer. The first challenge, however, was to get through secondary education and this would require money. The cost of school uniforms and books often prevented many of us from attending school.

I clearly remember my parents discussing these challenges one night.

"I am not stamping rupees at work," grumbled Appa. "I do not see how I can afford to put all these children through school. Better for the girls to marry young and let the brighter ones study," he said matter-of-factly. "It is so much easier to have children than to provide for them," he added with a sigh.

"Speak on your own behalf. Having children was not like milking cows for me. Now that we have them, it is your responsibility to provide for them," replied Amma tartly.

"Baskar is the brightest. He studies hard and shows the most promise."

"Maybe so, but Sheba has more perseverance than the others. She may not be the brightest but she has your stubbornness and will not give up without a fight."

"No," my father said flatly. "Baskar, then Jayakumar. Let the girls marry young. I am not a man of means and the factory can go either way now that plastics are preferred over palm products. We may have lean times ahead."

Appa's voice betrayed edginess and I could detect his frustration at not being able to provide for us the way he wished he could.

"Why only the boys, Appa? Let us give at least one of the girls a chance to be schooled."

"No. It is hard for the girls. They are not expected to progress in our society. Besides, an educated girl does not marry well among us."

"Pastor Stephen said there would be openings in the sponsorship program," Amma ventured.

"Yes, and how much will I need to pay to get Sheba in?" My

father was accustomed to the system of under-the-table gifts that procured a job, a promotion, or a place in school.

"Cha! Pastor Stephen will not allow that. They have a system. If you are poor you may be sponsored. If you have money you are not. It won't hurt. I am taking Sheba and Baskar to register on Sunday after church."

That Sunday was an important day for many families in Maduma Nagar and I suspect that many late night conversations took place like the one I have described above. Chopu, my close friend, was also present with her mother. I am certain that Pastor Stephen held the registration after his usual church service so that many of the non-churched people would attend his Sunday morning rooftop ministry. Registration was open to both Christians and non-Christians.

The previous Sunday, the pastor had dropped his usual 'preaching' voice and announced with his trademark grin, "I have good news! We have been given a quota and our children are to be registered into a child sponsorship program. Next Sunday after church, we will register children between the ages of eight and ten. Tell your friends and neighbors that this program is open to everyone, from all religions. Children who are registered will receive a *sponsor!*"

At the word 'sponsor', a buzz went through the crowd. I felt a sponsor must be awfully important because the word itself generated so much excitement. The pastor's enthusiasm for his 'quota' (another word I didn't quite grasp) was palpable. The excitement in Maduma Nagar was seen and heard everywhere. At the public well, in the market and along the footpaths, people were excitedly expressing their hopes for getting one or more of their children sponsored.

There was a problem though. The sponsorship organization had promised Pastor Stephen only fifty slots in their program. On the appointed Sunday, the church, which normally numbered nearly 100 adults and children, saw an overwhelming 350 people gathered in a colorful array of saris, umbrellas, and children. The owner of the restaurant below became quite agitated as the crowd surged towards the old rooftop. Finally, people were forced to assemble below, spilling over into the street in a raucous throng of hopeful parents and confused children.

A representative from the agency was on hand. I do not remember his name but I recall him standing patiently, a little overwhelmed at the turnout. His hair was oiled and combed straight back. He wore a clean pinstriped shirt with a red tie. His trousers were pressed with a neat crease down the middle, just like our school headmaster on assembly days. Unlike our headmaster, this man had a wonderful large beard, thick and black, and I wondered what it would be like to give it a tug. Like Pastor Stephen, his smooth skin was nearly coal black and contrasted wonderfully with his white teeth when he smiled.

After the service, Pastor Stephen gave the nice man an opportunity to speak. I was a little disappointed when the man apologized and said that he could not speak Tamil since he was from Bangalore, a city in the neighboring State of Karnataka. He spoke in English and our pastor translated for us. The man spoke with warmth and sincerity and I imagined him to be an excellent model of Jesus. I was certain that he loved children and I was surprised he did not have one of us in his arms.

Even so, he was not speaking so much to children but about children and a program that he hoped would bring opportunities to them.

"Only poor children can be registered," he began a little apologetically. "I know that many of you need support, but we have limited funds and can only take children from the poorest families. I will have to ask you a few personal questions like 'Where do you work', 'How much do you earn', and 'Where do you live?' to see if your child is eligible for sponsorship."

The crowd listened intently and the nice bearded man continued, "Once the children are registered, they will still have to wait a short time for a sponsor."

I perked up at the familiar word. My imagination went wild and I conjured up images of the sponsor coming personally to the congested streets of Maduma Nagar. Taking the sponsored child by the hand, he would escort him or her to a wonderful place where everybody wore clean clothes and little children did not die of dysentery or malnutrition. It was a fanciful thought but probably not too different from what the other children were imagining.

The agency man was still speaking.

"When your child is sponsored, our agency can help through the program at this church. The amount is not enough to support your family nor is it intended to provide the needs of all your children. We hope and pray this money will become a golden opportunity for your children. That it will be multiplied like the loaves and fishes beyond what we can give."

At this, many looked at each other and wondered aloud whether the program included distribution of bread and fish.

The speaker realized the confusion and hurried on. "I mean, the main purpose of the sponsorship program is to give your children a chance for a better future. Parents must ensure that their children attend all the special weekly sessions."

He looked serious and said, "You must use the money only for the purpose intended - school uniform, the school meal, books, and materials. If the money is misused or children are irregular, they will be terminated from the program."

At the word 'terminated' there was a collective gasp and then a hush. The word used in translation also meant 'to be executed'. Although appropriate in a technical sense, its usage caused confusion among the largely uneducated crowd.

When the agency man realized his mistake, he laughed. In fact, it was more of a chuckle, just like something I would have heard in my classroom. All at once, I liked the man for his childish laugh.

"No, no," he clarified with a smile. "Not 'executed' but dismissed from the program."

The business of registration was causing much excitement. I felt as if a traveling circus had come to Maduma Nagar. The speakers were using a public address system that rivaled the noisy traffic on the Perambur-Madras Highway. Down on the already crowded street, vendors briskly sold ice cream, orange-flavored soft drinks, fried bananas and fruit.

"Our goal is the same as your goal," continued the agency man. His smiling face suddenly became solemn and the crowd fell silent. "Could someone please tell me what you want for your children's lives?"

20

"I want my Chopu to become a doctor!" shouted my friend's mother.

"Wonderful! Do you also want your daughter to be in good health?"

"Can you make her a doctor?" Chopu's mother persisted.

"Anything is possible," replied the agency man nervously. He tried again. "Someone else please, what do you want for your children?"

"I want my boy to be a lawyer, can you make him a lawyer?"

The agency man decided to launch into his finale without further questions. He held up his hand with four fingers pointing skyward.

"I am holding up the 'crown' of the sponsorship program," he said.

His first finger pointed heavenward.

"Spiritual," he explained. "Your children will receive spiritual education. They will learn to respect all religions. Because we are Christians, we will tell them about God's law and about Jesus."

"Jesus is one of the gods we worship in our household. We even have a Jesus idol," interrupted a woman.

I knew this to be true since I had often seen images of Jesus or Mary respectfully enthroned with the Hindu pantheon.

"Be quiet," rejoined another angrily. "This man is not talking about that."

This kind of verbal exchange was normal and no one really paid any attention to it.

The agency man's second finger shot skyward.

"Social development," he bellowed. "We want your children to be good citizens. They will learn to respect their community, their elders and contribute to society. We will take them on special field trips, to the museum or government hall."

At this, there was another buzz of excitement as such free trips were unheard of, even at school.

A third finger went up and he said, "Education. Boys *and* girls

21

will need at least a high school education if they hope to provide for themselves and their future families."

I was glad he'd included girls.

"Students' marks will be monitored on a quarterly basis and, if possible, a special tutor will be provided for struggling students."

Finally his fourth finger shot up.

"Physical development. Immunization programs will be carried out. The children will be screened for diseases. If needed, sponsored children will be referred to a doctor."

It was becoming obvious that the crowd was getting restless and no longer in the mood to listen to details of the program. Children played and adults talked loudly to each other. They did not want to hear about the program. They had come only to register their children. If that were not possible, they wanted to go home and resume the myriad chores that always needed doing. Sensing this, the man from the agency said that he would now take applications for sponsorship.

"Just one last thing," he said hurriedly. "How many of you know what a sponsor is?"

That got the crowd's attention because like me, a lot of people were actually speculating.

The man continued.

"A sponsor is someone just like you. They are people who are not rich and do not have money to throw away. They all have one thing in common. They want to make a difference in the lives of children poorer than themselves. They give a little money every month so that we can have this program. It may mean that they and their families may not be able to do some things that they would like to, such as going to a cricket test match or eating a special meal at a restaurant. What can you give in return to the sponsor?"

"We are poor. That is why we need sponsors," shouted one woman. "If we had money to give, we would have given it to our own children."

There were cries and nods of assent.

"Yes, yes," nodded the agency man patiently, "but there is still something important that your children can give their sponsors."

The adults looked up guardedly. So, something was expected of them, of their children, in return for this sponsorship.

"Your children are learning to write," said the man. "They can write to their sponsors and tell them about their own lives. In this way, the sponsors will have the satisfaction of knowing that they are building a relationship. A bridge between two cultures can be built on the letters between your children and their sponsors."

"Are the sponsors able to speak our language? Even you cannot speak the Tamil tongue. How can they understand it in America or Australia?" asked one man bluntly.

The agency man gave an embarrassed laugh.

"No, your children may write in the language they speak. If they are able to write in English, they may do so. The letters that are not written in English will be translated for the sponsors. When the sponsors write letters we will translate those into your language so that the children will understand."

The crowd looked pleased but sensing that the time for talking was over, the agency man began the application process. As people queued up and jostled around the table, Pastor Stephen took the microphone and announced that a committee had been formed to ensure that there would be no bias in registering the children.

"The committee consists of parents from the different religious communities present in Maduma Nagar. The committee will select candidates for registration."

It was getting late. Some people left as word went around that families where both mother and father worked or in which the income was more than fifty rupees a day would not be enrolled. Others impatiently took their children by the arm and walked straight to the registration table. A sea of bright saris, waving arms, and the smell of perspiration deluged those who were trying to write down the information.

I watched the agency man who remained calm and focused on his work. He smiled patiently and seemed to hum to himself. Before long, my mother and I were standing in front of him. All at once, I felt as if his decree would result in our prosperity or ruin.

I found that he was humming a familiar hymn that I heard often

in church

Grant to us a deep compassion for thy children everywhere,
May we see our human family free from sorrow and despair,
And behold Thy kingdom glorious in our world so bright and fair.

"How old are you, child?"

To my surprise, his question was aimed at me and not my mother.

"Eight," I replied stiffly.

He stooped so that we were on eye level. In a friendly fashion, he continued to question me. He asked my name, what my Appa did for a living, and what I wanted to be when I grew up. To the last question I answered, as many children will in India, that I wanted to be a doctor. I quickly loosened up under this kind of friendly interrogation and felt that I had made a friend. A respected and older friend, but a friend nonetheless.

The odd thing was that he did not ask my mother any questions. He only spoke to me and, in doing so, affirmed my worth. I, a girl child, in a slum among thousands of slum communities in India.

"Just imagine, he listened to me!" I thought over and over.

That night, as I lay in bed, I gleefully repeated these words. So, Mr. Crenshaw, you will appreciate why I spun around in silly little girl circles when a month later, my brother told me the good news.

My friend Chopu and I compared notes the day after the registration. Unfortunately the agency man did not interview her but by one of the parent committee members and, unlike my interview, it was Chopu's mother who fielded the all-important questions.

To this day, I credit the kind man with the beard for boosting my sense of self-worth. I have tried in my own way to use his gift of truly *seeing* the child.

Two months after I was assigned a sponsor, I received your first letter, which has remained me with all these years.

3

April 21st, 1979

Dear Sheba,

How are you today? I hope that you and your family are well. It's April and in Iowa that means two things: rain, and crops to be sown. However, I'm no longer a farmer and that means I get to keep myself dry and indoor! Lately, I've been working at replacing most of the flooring at Farmer Thornton's place. Our town, or village as you might say, has only 640 people and is made up of mostly farmers, a few merchants, school teachers (five), and workers at a small dairy that processes the milk and dairy products around here. I wonder if the villages are so small in your country, Sheba?*

Anyway, this kind of work keeps me inside and mostly dry. (Unfortunately old Farmer Thornton's out planting and getting wet!) Thinking of old man Thornton (he's a year younger than me!), reminds me of a problem that farmers have in my country. He has four grown children who have all moved away to bigger cities. Seems the small towns are dull and young people want excitement.

In fact, Sheba, the same thing happened to me. Auntie Sue

25

Ellen and I were once farmers but when our children left home we were forced to lease out the farm and find other work. Thank God I am good with my hands. Guess it comes naturally from doing all the 'honey-do' lists Auntie Sue Ellen has given me over the years!

Our oldest son, Clayton, studied computer science and moved to St. Paul in a State called Minnesota, up north. He's married now and comes home during the holidays, but he's pretty much "citified" as we say. My daughter Tamara (Tambi in the picture I sent you last year) is married and lives in Des Moines. That's the capital of Iowa. Her husband works in the insurance industry while she works at home taking care of their children.

Our youngest boy, Randall (that's Randy next to Tambi in the picture) is in college doing a program called ROTC. He's learning how to be a soldier. He finishes college next year and plans to join the Marines. I am hoping that someday, when Randy is out of the Marines, he and I can run the farm again. The point is, Sheba, many farming families end up like this. The young ones move away and there's no one left to help the older folks run the farm. Perhaps, in another letter, I'll tell you about my farming days.

Auntie Sue Ellen is well and working to get her garden in order. She loves her garden, Sheba, and is planting many vegetables and fruits like she does every year. Since Auntie Sue Ellen's legs are not as strong as they once were, the garden gets smaller as the years go by. Most summer days, we eat fresh produce from the garden like lettuce, zucchini, corn, potatoes, peas, and tomatoes, to name a few. What we can't eat we give away. We put the extra produce (say, tomatoes) in a box and leave it outside the house with a sign saying 'Free tomatoes, help yourself'. People driving by stop and pick up what they need. Except for zucchinis. In our city it's said the only reason we lock our cars is so folks don't leave a load of zucchinis on the seat! What we can't eat or give away, Auntie Sue Ellen cans. We don't use tin cans but glass jars. The vegetables or fruit are poured in steaming hot and the jar lids sealed with wax for safe storage. We're hoping for warm weather since Auntie Sue Ellen is planting her strawberry and rhubarb plants today. That's good news to me since I believe rhubarb and strawberry pie is about as good a dish we'll get this side of heaven's gates.

I hope you're doing well at your studies, Sheba. We noticed that you've gotten some pretty good marks. I wouldn't worry too much about your math. It'll come.

Sheba, you've told me you live in a village on the outskirts of Madras. What kind of a village do you live in?

God bless and keep you dear one.

Love,

Clay and Auntie Sue Ellen Crenshaw

Thinking about your question, Mr. Crenshaw, my mind wanders back to a time, some twenty years ago.

To me, a village meant people. The small, mud-daubed huts that we lived in were secondary to the life that went on there. The village meant games of kabaddi, lattoo or top spinning, and hide-and-seek along the dusty paths that snaked around the crowded dwellings, trees, temples, and little vendor stalls of our community. It meant brushing my teeth and bathing at the community well with scores of other women, their saris secured sarong-style at chest level.

The village meant unbearably hot summer days when the only relief was a shady spot under a large banyan or bodi tree, its arching branches and luxuriant foliage forming a merciful barrier against the fierce sun. Under that green canopy, we children would lie on our backs near dogs and cats, whose elastic bodies stretched to ward off the heat.

The village also meant the roar of relentless monsoon rains that brought floods, fearful as fires to slum dwellers. I remember the story I was often told about the time my father held me high over his head to prevent me from drowning in the rising floodwaters. At that time, I was still an infant and my parents' only child.

Fifty years ago, Maduma Nagar was a village. In those days, it was considered far from Madras, being separated from the city by numerous dusty roads and canals that flowed inland from the Bay of Bengal.

Actually, Maduma Nagar has never been a village in the sense of a small cluster of homes surrounded by fields of rice, lentils, and coconut trees. But the word we use in Tamil is 'nagar', which means a community or village.

Those of us who live in Maduma Nagar consider ourselves a community. If community development specialists visited us, they would probably call our village an urban blight. To put it simply, what began as a settlement of low caste squatters grew into a slum.

As part of the Perambur Township, Maduma Nagar lies on the fringes of Chennai, the capital of Tamil Nadu.

We, in Tamil Nadu, like to think of ourselves as a progressive

State. One of our famous leaders, a bold man named Periyar, applied the teachings of Mahatma Gandhi (his contemporary) to local law. He made caste distinctions illegal. Even calling a person paraiyar or low-caste could earn you a lawsuit. He also banned families from spending large amounts on a young girl's coming-of-age function. Dowry, which amounts to buying a groom, was also deemed illegal. Sadly, the last two customs are still widely practiced.

You would know our city as 'Madras' but it was recently renamed 'Chennai'. Apparently, the name reflects the city's origins.

Maduma Nagar has existed for over sixty years. It was established hastily and was the subject of much controversy in the mid-1940s, during the turbulent days of India's Independence movement. Squatters and people looking to buy land cheaply, rushed into an area, which had no infrastructure to handle the influx.

Their joy is joy of all the world, they see; thus more
The learners learn to love their cherished lore.

The Kurral

❧ 4 ❧

My paternal grandfather, Albert Sunderraj, loved telling us about the early days of our settlement.

In those days, Maduma Nagar had little going for it. Twenty kilometers north of Madras, it was simply seen as a refuge for ragtag, low-caste settlers who swarmed into this low-lying, flood-prone area.

Maduma Nagar takes its name from a large channel of water that drains into two swampy lakes. Monsoon rains swell the lakes until the channel surrounds the community so that it looks like an island under siege.

During the 1940s, land was cheap on the outskirts of Madras. A small plot of land could be bought for a thousand rupees. Those were hope-filled days for the downtrodden. Ownership of land near the growing industrial center of Madras would be their way out of poverty - or so they thought.

Those who couldn't afford to buy land simply squatted on it. Many families were eventually driven out by the floodwaters, but others endured and earned the right to remain on their land.

The old people recall the early days as a time when educated people stayed away from Maduma Nagar. Many are ashamed to admit that our community had such a poor reputation. It was an unruly place with infamous rogues and gangs. Any bus passing through the area was fair game for rock throwers. In the event of a local incident, such as the firing of a worker at the nearby tractor factory, buses would be stopped, passengers pulled from the safety of their conveyance, the bus burnt and the hapless travelers beaten.

Apart from the traffic and drab government housing projects, not much has changed in Maduma Nagar. I've heard people comment that our community is moving from poor to lower-middle class. But those living in Maduma Nagar simply consider it an established slum. What began as mud homes with thatched roofs grew into a crowded community of tiny concrete houses, oven-hot under their tin ceilings.

Fatalists call our community a prison for those guilty of the crime of being born poor and sentenced to lifelong poverty. Whatever others say, I knew it as home, and the people who lived around me were my treasured neighbors.

Perhaps I should tell you how our family came to be here.

As newlyweds, my paternal grandparents, Albert and Aruna Sunderraj, came to Maduma Nagar in search of a better life. They had been married in the courtyard of a poor parish in Madras. For his wedding, my grandfather borrowed a clean shirt from a friend who had three shirts and was considered quite wealthy. Grandmother Aruna was dressed in the sari she reserved for church; her other sari was for everyday wear. These two articles of clothing made up the bulk of her wardrobe. The sum total of their possessions could be carried by hand or borne atop their heads like an awkward umbrella.

Before his marriage, Grandfather had worked as a daily wage laborer for wealthy old Mr. Advani who owned two ox-drawn carts. The ox carts were hired out to haul bricks for construction, move a family's possessions, or relocate canal sludge to higher ground.

Ox cart driving was then, as it is today, a tedious job. The life of the laborer is intrinsically linked to that of the poor ox. If one or the other should fall ill or be injured, the other suffers from no work and, therefore, no food.

As his father's father had done before him, young Albert would rise before dawn. He would feed the tired-looking ox before hitching it to the wooden cart. Albert would then grease the wheels and set off on another day of drudgery. The only highlights were the intermittent brushes with death caused by lorry drivers who were possessive with the narrow roadway.

As he hitched the ox to the smooth wooden yoke, Grandfather noticed the animal's coarse hide. It was stretched over its bones like shrunken leather to reveal gaunt ribs. The weary beast moved slowly and could not shoulder heavy loads making multiple trips necessary even for small jobs. Tedious trips became long days that stretched to wearisome nights. Grandfather, barely out adolescence, sat awkwardly on top of the payload and dreamed of his escape from poverty.

By the age of eighteen, a young man was expected to work, marry and fill the niche carved out for him by fate and our caste system. For the low castes, the saying 'life is short' had harsh connotations. At that time, a man's average life span was about forty-four years and did not allow the luxury of a prolonged period of youthfulness as is enjoyed in many western countries. Instead, there were demands to adhere to a code prescribed by a poet long ago. It goes something like this:

There's a fancy some lean to
And others hate
That when sweet youth is ended, begins
New work for the soul in another state
Then it strives, gets weary, loses and wins
Until the strong and the weak, embraced in turmoil
Repeat in large what they practiced in small
Only the scales are to be changed, that's all.

One evening, after a long hot day spent riding atop a load of jute bags swollen with rice, Grandfather returned as usual to Mr. Advani's residence. After the evening meal, Mr. Advani always sat on the upper floor to enjoy the coolest part of the day. Stray breezes would rustle his newspaper. Usually the newspaper came delayed by a couple of days. It would pass from one reader to the next who in turn would enlighten his neighbors of the latest news of Madras and beyond.

Grandfather attempted to retreat stealthily, too exhausted

to even look up and inquire about the next day's work. Perhaps God was watching over our family that evening for Mr. Advani was watching Grandfather from the rooftop. When he saw Grandfather walking away he called out, "Albert! Are you not interested in tomorrow's labors?"

"No, sir. I'm too tired and tomorrow I'll rest. I must take my mother to church in the morning," replied Grandfather turning to go again.

"Suit yourself," shrugged Mr. Advani.

And then suddenly he called out again.

"Oh, Albert! Come here and read this."

Grandfather froze. In the background, he could hear the clatter from the kitchen. The smell of dinner being prepared aroused a painful response from the pit of his empty stomach.

"Sir, you know I cannot read. I haven't had a day's schooling in my life."

"Oh, yes, quite right," replied Mr. Advani unsmilingly yet a little pleased that his intellectual superiority was on display. "However, you must hear about a place near Perambur. You know, Perambur? The place where the British have built those factories north of Madras?"

Grandfather was more than aware of Perambur. The thought of a job at one of the factories tugged longingly at his heart just as the smell of food tugged at his stomach. Those factory workers were taken care of for life. Employment benefits made it possible for a man to be married, have a family, and make plans beyond a day's labor.

But Grandfather did not want to torture himself with fanciful dreams. To get a factory job required a basic education. Albert could not even read or write his own name. And, sometimes, it required bribing an unscrupulous manager.

Mr. Advani continued, "There are many low caste people flocking there to buy swamp land!" he said, chortling in his low guttural way. "Some are even squatting on government land hoping the local township will deed it over to them after Independence. They run there thinking more is the fruit of much!"

Mr. Advani laughed out loud, his great pneumatic body rippling with sinister delight. My grandfather watched the old man's white moustache quiver with animation. For a fleeting moment, Grandfather felt a spark of hope ignite in his heart. But just as quickly, it was doused by the crushing realization that he had nothing with which he could purchase this fleeting dream. Mr. Advani knew this too.

My gentle grandfather bit his lip and merely replied, "I am poor and uneducated and cannot even afford a bribe to the foreman. They will never consider me for work there."

Mr. Advani stood on his balcony, like a raja holding court. Looking down at Albert, his plump hands moved up and down like a merchant's weighing scales.

"Big work makes small work!" was his quixotic reply.

My grandfather went home that night, deeply upset. Why had that foolish old man ridiculed him? He was just a poor uneducated youth. Lying on the floor of his mother's small hut, he found he couldn't fall asleep. The hut was at the rear of the house of a government worker where his mother worked as a minor servant among a staff of five. Grandfather got up and walked among the mango and tamarind trees surrounding the house.

"I knew then how the prophets of old must have felt," he would tell us years later. "I felt as if there was a fire burning inside me."

It was the fire of desire. The desire to be free and choose his way in life.

"Oh Lord," he prayed, "Give me the opportunity to escape this tiger-like grip of poverty. Deliver me just as you delivered Joseph from slavery and poverty."

Poverty, his young mind reasoned, was even worse than slavery. And no great social movement could free him from its invisible shackles. Bound by poverty, he could not study, plan, save, or even dream of possibilities. He could only work for meager wages that would sustain his life from day-to-day. And with each new day, the cycle of despair would be repeated.

That night, as the crows flitted in and out of the tamarind

trees, Grandfather said that for the first time in his life he had faith. In his simple, unassuming way he said it was not the kind of faith that saves but the kind of faith that moves.

He pictured Joseph as he had seen him in the color posters used by pastors and missionaries. Joseph in his colorful robes. Joseph in rags, asking God for deliverance from prison. Joseph in prison for seven years. Albert had been poor for nearly three times as long as that. Surely God would deliver him!

As he continued his midnight stroll, Grandfather came upon a goat. It placidly munched an over-ripe papaya whose fermented fragrance filled the air. The goat reminded him of someone. Mr. Advani! He, with his comical moustache, his portly belly, and his chubby hands moving up and down as he chanted cryptically, "Big work makes little work."

And then, in a flash, Grandfather understood a basic economic principle. Big work makes little work! A place with large factories would have plenty of ancillary factories and businesses. There would surely be a flow of employment, even for daily-hires like him!

The story of his migration from Madras to Perambur is an arduous one. It involved days of toil and fasting and a mother's sacrificial love to save the amount he needed for his journey.

As he walked out of his old home towards his new one, he was hit by the realization that he wasn't just covering a geographical distance. He was crossing the lines laid down by ages of discrimination. He felt as if angry and suspicious eyes were watching his every step. Silent, glowering faces seemed to challenge his audacious exodus, as though by a mere 42-kilometer walk he could shake off a centuries-old caste system.

After two years of hard work, Grandfather had saved up enough to marry Grandmother Aruna. They returned to Maduma Nagar in Perambur Township, with her dowry of two goats and a set of stainless steel drinking cups and dishes.

June 6, 1979

Dear Sheba,

fternoon greetings to you from Sioux City, Crofton, Iowa.
I received your letter recently and I must say that Auntie
and I both enjoyed the picture that you drew and sent us.
Even though your words were few, you more than made up for it
by drawing a beautiful picture. It looks as though you have drawn
a village well. There are people all around and some are carrying
buckets. Those buckets look heavy and some have water splashing
out! It also looks as though people are bathing at the well. What
a busy place that must be! Do you go there every day, Sheba? We
like your picture very much and have put it on our refrigerator
where we put only important things like family pictures and emergency telephone numbers.

Last week Auntie Sue Ellen and I did something very exciting! We loaded our old Dodge station wagon and drove to Des
Moines to visit our kids and grandchildren. There is nothing more
exciting than taking off on a road trip on a warm June morning. Country roads are a pleasure to drive on. Wherever there's a
farmhouse or small community, there's a group of trees that help

to cool the homes with shade and provide a break from the winds that blow across the prairie. In some places there are rest stops with trees and at one such spot Auntie Sue Ellen and I stopped for lunch. We had fried chicken, biscuits, and iced tea. It was a very peaceful time.

We made it safely to Tambi's (I told you about her in an earlier letter) house in Des Moines, 170 miles down the road. We spent the weekend with her and her family. Did I tell you that she's had a baby? That brings her kids up to four! Daniel James is six, Travis Lee is four, Sabrina is two and now Isabelle! They certainly have their hands full and, between you and me, Sheba, I think this is the reason why Tambi and her husband like having us over. When we arrived, we took up our duties as grandparents, which we enjoy. I love to play with the children though I don't have the energy I used to have for playing! Auntie helps with the cooking and we usually give Tambi and her husband (did I tell you his name is Dan?) a chance to go out and escape the house!

After church, we had lunch at Country Bob's steakhouse and came back home. I got sleepy part way so Auntie drove the rest of the way home.

Well Sheba, that's my letter for now. I hope you have grandparents, Sheba. Why don't you tell me about them in your next letter?

With love to your family and friends,

Clay and Auntie Sue Ellen Crenshaw

His skin was smooth, pink like the belly of a pig. It glowed after he bathed."

My maternal great-grandmother, Thangamal, began a story about her husband, Robert Shaw Cunningham, a British soldier who served in India long before the country's independence in 1947.

The others were asleep, but my little brother Sammy lay under the mosquito net, eyes bright and head perched upon his hands in hopeful expectation.

"He had sandy-colored hair and strange eyes. They were blue, and such a piercing blue that at first I could not get used to them. It was like looking into water," she said wistfully.

"He was a good man but we rarely saw him," she continued. "Sometimes he was called away for months on foreign campaigns. His time in Afghanistan must have been terrifying for after that campaign I noticed he drank more and more. Did you know that he was in charge of the regiment that was sent to Perambur to quell the riots at the railway factories? He knocked some sense into the heads of those rabble-rousers trying to cause disruption among the factory workers and..."

"Did he shoot any rabble-rousers?" interrupted Sammy excitedly.

"I don't know if he shot anybody," quavered great-grandmother.

"Tell us about his gun!"

Sammy enjoyed any story that involved adventure.

"I only remember, Sammy, that it was very heavy and as large as a tree trunk. He often came home with his equipment. His uniform was heavy with ribbons and medals. He must have been a very successful soldier as he was quite popular with those above and below him in rank. When he arrived home, he would first put his large rifle in a corner of the house. The dark wood and hard black metal of the weapon frightened me and I did not like to have it in the house!"

"Did you ever see him shoot his rifle?" Sammy asked, not willing to leave the story at that.

"Heavens no! And I am glad of that for I was told it was as loud as a cannon! He not only had a rifle but leather gloves, a pistol holster, and a revolver that he kept hidden. He never allowed anyone to touch it. He kept all these things in a locked chest that no one dared open."

"But Grandma, what about the big knife?" Sammy had always been curious about this legendary knife.

"Oh yes, he had a large kukri, the Gurkha knife that was given to him during the Afghanistan campaign."

Sammy's eyes brightened as he dreamed of finding the prized kukri.

Knowing my younger brother, he imagined himself waving it wildly over his head while chasing brigands and thieves from our neighborhood.

"Don't you have any of his things anymore Grandmother Thangamal?" Sammy asked persistently.

"Oh, Sammy, you sound so much like your Grandfather Shoban. He too was curious about such matters. It's not good for you and will only end in your ruin!" scolded Grandmother Thangamal.

"Shoban was fascinated by his father's chest of military gear. He made his father promise that it someday it would be his. I don't know why men are so captivated by weapons and war!" she said almost desperately.

There was a dark secret behind her story. We children weren't supposed to know but the truth seeps out, somehow. Thangamal, my frail, eighty-nine-year-old great-grandmother, had not been the wife but the mistress of Robert Shaw Cunningham.

Robert was born in 1887 into a well-to-do British family who lived in Madras during the waning years of the Raj. His father, a civil servant, arrived in India in the late 19th century. He became Chief Collector for the districts in north Madras. Robert's mother was a social creature whose life revolved around events that she was either organizing or attending. She didn't limit herself to the foreign community but organized the servants' lives and quite a few charitable projects for the Anglican Church.

Grandmother Thangamal was a servant, an assistant chambermaid, who worked in the Cunningham household. A faded photograph shows that she was very beautiful. It seemed inevitable that she should catch the eye of young Robert. What began as innocent inquiries about the local Tamil dialect by the curious Robert grew into long conversations, clandestine walks, and a secret romance. For secret it had to be; such a relationship would never be condoned by either family. The young couple pledged undying devotion to one another knowing that their love was doomed by society's standards. Robert could have returned to England to attend a prestigious college, but gave it up because of his love for Thangamal. Instead, he enlisted in a local regiment.

Their secret romance would have dire consequences through the generations.

Robert's mother was furious when she discovered that he was supporting a local girl on his soldier's income. Enlisting the aid of his father and his Company commandant, she pressured him to take a wife. Not Thangamal, of course, but one from the British community. Robert bowed to the pressure but couldn't give up Thangamal. He continued to live a life of deception, maintaining two households.

And then, a baby was born to Thangamal and Robert; a beautiful son whom they named Shoban. But not even the arrival of the baby could disguise the fact that Robert felt torn between two worlds. By the time Grandfather Shoban was three years old, Robert's visits to Thangamal's small rented quarters were becoming infrequent.

And then, just before Lord Mountbatten, last Viceroy to India, conceded independence through an imperial decree to the Indian Parliament, my great-grandfather Robert Shaw Cunningham took his English wife and their two children back to England and never returned to India.

"He left so suddenly," said Grandmother Thangamal softly, the sadness still present in her voice even after so many years.

"It wasn't a pleasant scene. He sent a Gurkha from the camp to clear out his possessions. He was too ashamed to come himself and tell me he was returning to England."

Shoban, my grandfather, was twelve years old when he returned home that day to find that his father's possessions had been removed from their little home. All that remained was the wooden chest. He would never see or hear from his father again.

"Grandmother Thangamal, why didn't you lodge a complaint with the Army? What Robert did to you was criminal!" My normally reserved mother evidently felt the injustice keenly.

"I was tempted to go to his commanding officer and cause a scene but it wasn't likely that anybody would listen to a worn out domestic servant. We were as numerous as kitchen rats then. I held my dignity in silence while he left in shame. I could bear the insult, but Shoban felt deeply disgraced. He couldn't face his friends. The day his father left was his last day at school. He never studied again."

Robert had ordered the Gurkha to leave behind the chest and its contents as he had promised them to Shoban.

"Grandfather Shoban got the gun?" piped up Sammy excitedly.

"Enough, Sammy," snapped my mother.

Surprised at her harshness, Sammy lay down quietly.

Grandmother Thangamal stared blankly into the dark recesses of the now quiet room.

"I saw Shoban walking with his two friends. I can see still see it now. It was the last carefree day he ever had. They were kicking up the dust and spinning a lattoo between them. The boys were oblivious to the heat of the afternoon. I felt so alone, knowing that it would fall on me to give the boy the bad news. Even our neighbors in the row of houses on either side disappeared into their dark rooms, sensing that an evil spirit had fallen upon the place. I didn't know how to handle the situation. Should I stay quiet and hope that he wouldn't notice the missing things? Would he notice and bear his grief in silence? I was torn sitting there, watching my son walk into the trap that fate had set for him. One part of me wanted to run to him, there in the dusty road, hold him and cry on his shoulder to seek my comfort. Instead I sat in the oppressive shade of the doorway and watched him approach."

Great-grandmother's face contorted in pain as she recalled

her next words.

"'He's left. Your father's gone back to England', I heard myself say he neared the door. Shoban flinched as though I'd had struck him. In silence, he walked to his mat and lay down. At that moment, all the light went out of that boy's life."

Her voice faded in the darkness. I felt her soul's anguish fill my heart like the odor of wood-fire smoke that clings to every nook and cranny of the kitchen.

Grandmother Thangamal continued. "We had nowhere to go after that sad day. We couldn't afford to pay the rent without his father's support."

"What did you do?" I asked anxiously.

This was the first time she had told us the story of her abandonment. I wanted to hear the whole story and was afraid the old woman might meander to another unrelated story as she often did.

"I could only do what I had learned as a child. I made idly."

Idly! That staple Tamilian breakfast item. A bland, palm-sized cake made from rice flour, often eaten with a curry called sambar.

"We moved into a small room that my father built for me in his little house. I had saved up two hundred and fifty rupees from the money that Robert gave me as support. With his final installment, I bought flour, some wood for fuel and a few utensils to set me up in business. I was tempted to sell the few possessions that he had left for Shoban. But I reasoned that the boy had nothing else to remember him by so I put the chest aside."

In India, Mr. Crenshaw, ancestors are not nameless ghosts. They live on in their deeds, whether for good or bad. Each is remembered in a fragmented way, like scraps of newsprint blown along on a windy day. Grandmother Thangamal, the brave survivor; Robert Shaw Cunningham, deserter of his family. I sometimes wonder what my fragment will say. I hope it will read, 'She cared enough to tell the story'. I see the flutter of newsprint for the grandfather I never knew. It reads, "Died of rejection" and serves as the final sad note on the history of Shoban.

Grandmother Thangamal continued.

"They say there is no greater power than fate but I say there is no greater power than the will to live! Every morning Shoban and I were up before dawn. He gathered firewood and fetched water while I prepared iddly and sambar. Before light, we were on the crowded railroad platforms selling iddly to hungry travelers."

I wonder how Shoban felt as he watched the travelers whose lives seemed so full and interesting.

By now all the children except myself were asleep. Amma got up abruptly and began to adjust the mosquito net. She seemed to be looking for chores to do and I sensed that the story was coming to a close and that, for some reason, she didn't want to hear the end.

Grandfather Shoban grew up and married. He worked for daily hire and earned enough for the family. But the tragedy of his life was that he never found healing for his childhood hurt. The bitterness scourged a mean streak in his character. He found escape in alcohol. His wife, a delicate wisp, died a few years after their last daughter was born.

And there, Grandmother Thangamal stopped. Though I instinctively knew that there was more to be told, I felt she had exhausted her reserves of emotional strength and couldn't go on.

It was my mother who continued, in hushed tones, after Grandmother Thangamal lay down.

"I feel you need to know the truth, Sheba," she whispered. "The torch of truth, however bitter, has to be passed on to the next generation."

My mother too, returned home one day, to find that her father had left without warning. But not to England.

On the verge of collapse because of his abuse of an illegally distilled potent rice liquor called sura, and unable to work because of his physical and emotional disabilities, Shoban became severely depressed. One afternoon, he opened his father's chest of treasured possessions and drew out a lasting reminder of the father for whom he yearned.

At the age of thirty-two, Shoban shot himself through the head.

The bullet that shattered his head was his last desperate attempt to permanently remove the pain of rejection.

He left behind his mother Thangamal and four daughters, my mother the oldest at eight. My family was cast upon the world with no resources except their strength and a fierce determination to survive in a harsh environment. Like her father before her, my mother never returned to school. Unlike her father, she kept her light alive with her deep love for her grandmother and her strong faith in God.

November 3, 1980

Dear Sheba,

I *trust you received our birthday card and gift. A tenth birthday is very important. Here, in America, boys often receive their first baseball glove and bat on their tenth birthday. For girls, it's the age when they start thinking about nice clothes and such. That is why Auntie went to Woolworth's and selected the blue pinafore especially for you. I hope you like it. In your last letter, you told us about your school and playground. So we thought you might like something special to wear when you play.*

We are happy to hear that your family is well and that God has answered prayer for your grandmother. Sheba, I hope you never forget how important it is to pray for your grandparents. I believe it's most likely the prayers of grandchildren that keep their grandparents alive, though I suspect your guardian angel could also use some support from grand folks like us as well!

We are well on this side of the world and thank the good Lord that we have our health. I almost lost mine last Tuesday, Sheba. As I stepped out of my workshop, I looked up at some geese flying overhead. The next thing I knew I was flat on my back, looking at

45

stars! I had forgotten that the concrete walk was covered with ice. My feet just flew right out from under me. And when Auntie rushed out to help me up, all I could say was "Look at the geese, look at the geese!"

We're able to laugh about this incident now, but I'm afraid I gave Auntie a bit of a scare at the time. Ice is a problem we have every winter, Sheba. It's everywhere. On the roads, in the plumbing, even in your hair if you're not careful. You're lucky that Madras doesn't have the ice problem. Of course, Auntie told me I should have scattered salt on the walkways (that makes them less slippery). I didn't and paid the price. But, Sheba, I have found you can't do everything at once and I just didn't get around to doing it!

My children are fine. I told them the story about the geese and the ice and they had a good laugh but also made me promise to be careful on the ice.

Bob and Eunice Thornton have agreed to come over on Saturday to help us wallpaper our house. They papered their house so we'll be glad for their experience. Auntie agreed that since she has experience in making chicken and dumplings we'd have dinner together afterwards. Sounds like a good arrangement, doesn't it Sheba?

Well dear, it sure is good to have friends like the Thorntons. I hope you have some close friends, Sheba. Why don't you write us a letter about your best friend?

Take care precious one. We pray for you every morning. Hey, how about that? Titus, our old basset hound just looked up at me as though to say "hello". Hello from Titus, Sheba!

Clay and Auntie Sue Ellen Crenshaw

I close my eyes and think of the many friends I had while growing up in Maduma Nagar. I am thankful that though money is scarce in the slums, children are not!

I see two faces bobbing like balloons. But instead of floating in the sky, they bob on the surface of water, deep inside a cool dark well.

Peering down the village well on hot afternoons, Chopu and I often imagined a secret stairway leading down to the water, ten meters below. The uneven walls of the well were carpeted with moss punctuated by leafy sprigs of fern. A delightful mossy smell filled our nostrils.

We loved draping ourselves over the well wall. We would insert our feet, claw-like, into the crevices of the outer rocks of the wall, oblivious to the insects or creatures lurking inside. Peering into the darkness, we could see the shimmering surface of the water. If the light was right, we could see two heads reflected like balloons floating in the water far below. We named the balloons our twin sisters and called out our wishes to them.

"What's your name?" I called out to the twins below and back came the reply, "What's your name, what's your name?" We giggled down and the twins giggled up.

It was rare for us to spend time undisturbed at our wishing well. Normally, it was one of the busiest, noisiest spots in the community. None of our homes had running water, Mr. Crenshaw, and even today it's rare to find a tap in a slum home. Early in the morning, people cleaning their teeth and bathing surrounded the well. Once the men went to work and the children were sent to school, the women would congregate at the well to wash clothes and fill up their kodams, pear-shaped water pots. As they scrubbed and rinsed, the women chattered non-stop, exchanging gossip. Once they'd finished at the well, they would heft the kodams on to their hips or heads and file back to their homes. Later in the afternoon, when the sun was hot and fierce, we girls would wander to the well after school for some fun.

I can't remember when I first met my best friend, Chopu.

She was one of those friends who I grew up with and has no beginning in my memory. In fact, it was only when we started school that I discovered her name was actually Aruna Gupta.

"Sheba Victoria!" said the teacher as she marked the attendance register. Everyone turned and looked at me. But when the teacher barked, "Aruna Gupta", we all looked blankly at each other until Chopu raised her scrawny arm in response.

In the village, she was simply known as Chopu, which is Tamil for toy or doll. It was an appropriate name. Her most prominent feature was a button nose that would have been at home on a doll. Chopu's parents were transplants, a North Indian Hindu family from New Delhi. Her father came to work at the local railway factory. After a few years, he was made redundant but they had no money to return to home. Her father found work as a laborer in a tannery and they stayed on in Maduma Nagar.

Head tilted back in a fit of giggles, and a mouth always missing teeth, is how I remember little Chopu. A bundle of activity, she was often out and about in the village and welcomed in nearly every house thanks to her happy demeanor.

One morning, during our summer holidays, we went down to the well to chat with our 'twins'. Few people were out in the blistering sun.

"What will I be when I grow up, twin sister?" Chopu called down to the floating head.

"What did she reply?" I whispered, not wanting to disturb the oracle of the well.

"I think she said, 'You are going to be the wife of the Collector!'" whispered Chopu excitedly, her eyes as large as pomegranates.

"I'll check again," I hissed. Leaning further into the well I shouted, "Sister, sister, who will Chopu marry?"

"And," Chopu added hastily, "how many children will she have and how old will she be when she marries?"

In her eagerness to address the oracle, Chopu leaned so far that her feet nearly went up over her head. I grabbed her threadbare shirt just in time and pulled her back. We both sat back hard and stared at each other, contemplating the near tragedy.

Breathing hard, Chopu whispered, "What did she say?"

I retorted angrily that the twins said there was not enough room for three sisters at the bottom of the well.

"Besides," I added, "you will never marry if you fall into the well!"

The clanging of metal washtubs startled us and we both jumped up.

"You girls have no business playing here at the well. Get out of my way and let the women who need the water for work have some room!"

Large Mrs. Jyothimani waddled to the well, her washtubs and bundle of washing making her even more ungainly than usual. She came late to the well because the other women had recently ostracized her. A gossip was fine but a gossip that tried to cause splits was not tolerated. Mrs. Jyothimani was of the latter ilk and as such found herself cold-shouldered.

Panting, she plunked her burdens by the well and flapped her hands at us as if shooing away pesky crows. We looked down and giggled since the violent movement had made her tremendous bulk wobble threateningly.

"I hope you are not throwing rubbish into the well! Young girls like you ought to be home helping your mothers. Don't you have something better to do?" she rasped.

Her glares made us forget us our giggles. Holding hands, we fled with her scornful voice calling after us, "Good, good. Get on home with you and help your mothers do their chores!"

We ran and turned down a dirt lane where old Mr. Venugopal lived. His villa, a bleached cream in the late morning sun, looked inviting due to the abundance of shade trees that encircled his garden. The dogs that normally guarded his gate reposed lazily on the hot and dusty footpath. To my chagrin, Chopu stopped in front of the gate. From the look on her face, I knew she was planning something I wouldn't like.

"Chopu!" I whined, hoping to distract her, "We have to fetch the milk my mother wants for Kalyani. Have you forgotten?" I dangled the brass milk container in front of her face. "We've already wasted so much time at the well!"

49

"Oh, your baby sister won't starve if we're a little delayed," was the careless reply.

"Look, Sheba! There are lots of men in Mr. Venugopal's house. Must be an important meeting. Let's find out what it's about."

"Chopu!" I exclaimed.

But it was too late. She had already darted around the dozing dogs and was through the small gate.

A large crowd of men stood in front of the doorway blocking her view of what was going on inside. Chopu dashed around the corner and headed to the rear of the house. I sighed and darted in after her.

A voice came from behind me. "What are you doing here, Sheba?"

I skidded to a halt under the shade of the lush pink and white bougainvilleas.

Turning nervously I saw it was one of Mr. Venugopal's servants, a neighbor of ours. I wondered what to reply since I knew that any misbehavior would be reported to my father. Mr. Venugopal, as community president gave counsel on a variety of subjects. Appa would not be amused if he found I'd been up to mischief in Mr. Venugopal's compound.

At that moment, Chopu's head appeared around the corner of the house.

"We saw some tamarind pods on the ground under the tree. May we collect them?" Chopu's button nose danced merrily above a toothy grin.

The maid nodded and continued sweeping.

I joined Chopu behind the house and we rooted around the old tamarind tree. A brood of chickens scratched along with us, hoping to find the juicy worms and insects that feasted on the fallen fruit.

Our mouths watered as we peeled back the tamarind pods to get at the sweet and sour gooey fruit. To our disappointment, the seeds were too rotten to eat.

"Chee!" spat Chopu in disgust.

Looking around, she spotted a sapota tree laden with sumptuous fruit. She shinnied up a few branches and plucked as many sapotas as we could both hold. We seated ourselves in the shade under an open window. We could clearly hear Mr. Venugopal's gentle singsong voice. Peeling the thin leathery skins, we slurped the sweet syrupy fruit in silence, spitting the seeds at the chickens.

"What are they talking about?" Chopu mumbled, a trickle of sticky juice running down her chin.

I discovered later, that the men had been discussing the building of a new weir on the large canal that dissected our community. Since it was April, the canal was nearly bone-dry. It was a good time to make repairs and prepare for the monsoon rains. By building the new weir, the men hoped to avert or at least reduce the annual flooding that our community received.

At that moment, however, I peered through a crack between the opened shutter and the window frame and tried to see who was present. I could see Mr. Venugopal's back as he sat behind a large wooden table. Neatly arranged on the table were his books, some letters, and a kerosene lamp. The invigorating smell of freshly brewed coffee hung in the air. Mr. Venugopal sipped his coffee from a stainless steel tumbler while listening intently to a man who spoke in an aggressive whine.

"Mr. Venugopal," he said, "I am not understanding why it is that working people like myself must be taking time to dig like common laborers. I've got to be out continually selling shoes and in this traffic it can take hours to get from Perambur to Poonamallee. Why can we not simply have the lower castes do the labor? As it is, all they do is lie about all day."

A murmur rumbled through the room. Except for the speaker Mr. Sathyamurthy, most of those present were long-standing residents of Maduma Nagar and the surrounding localities. New to our village, Mr. Sathyamurthy had purchased some land that was adjacent to the proposed weir. Newcomers were little trusted and his talk this morning wasn't making him any more popular.

His faded blue lungi hung precariously around his expansive waist. His loose, long-sleeved, white cotton shirt bore evidence that he was perspiring heavily. His moustache was most odd. It thrust out from under his nose like a wire brush and I speculated on whether it was actually a moustache or an explosion of nasal hair that had extended far beyond its natural domain.

Mr. Venugopal placed his tumbler deliberately on the table and stood up. His baldpate shone in the sunlight and he glared at Mr. Sathyamurthy through thick-rimmed glasses. There was a hush in the room. Everyone present, barring Mr. Sathyamurthy, knew that Mr. Venugopal was a formidable opponent who had won much harder battles than this.

"Yes, I have heard your reasoning," he began. "No doubt you are thinking of the saying, 'keep clear of a bull with long horns, a widow without shame, and an educated sutra'. But Mr. Sathyamurthy, you are making my blood boil! You bought your way into this community with property, while your neighbors endured floods and fire to maintain their land. Today, we are meeting to agree on a plan to collectively prevent the flooding and protect our houses, yes even your own house, Mr. Sathyamurthy!"

His opponent tried to speak but Mr. Venugopal silenced him with a wave of his hand.

"Mr. Sathyamurthy, allow someone who is much older than all present here, to tell you that some of these so-called sutras, the lower castes, are more educated than you or I. Even so, we will all work and get our hands dirty to protect the whole community, high and low caste, if you choose to make the distinction!"

Mr. Sathyamurthy attempted a feeble rejoinder. "I didn't mean that the sutras should do all the work..."

A low and dangerous murmur from those assembled caused him to fade off. Mr. Sathyamurthy didn't seem to realize that he was up against a Brahmin who had fought all his life for a casteless society.

Seventy-six-year-old Mr. Venugopal was almost a mythical figure in our community. Born a Brahmin and raised to follow complicated rituals of diet, hygiene, and purification, he turned his back on his high-caste status as a young man. He joined the ranks of those rare reformers who dedicate their lives to the ideals of an egalitarian society. It was evident, though, that despite his dedicated efforts, thousands of years of tradition and the repressive caste system would not be undone in a single generation.

In the 1940s, he worked as a manager at the Perambur railroad factory that produced rail cars. By the end of his career, he was President of the Railway Workers Union, South India. Not an insignificant achievement, Mr. Crenshaw! He used to proudly say that the railroad was the fulcrum on which the lever of India's industrial revolution turned. A statement that makes sense to me now but baffled me as a child. After he retired, he settled down in our area in a gracious villa and served as the leader, the chief elder, of our community.

Holding Mr. Sathymurthy in a steady gaze, Mr. Venugopal began to relate an incident from the pre-Independence years when he worked as a Union Station Chief at the Indian Railways.

"When I worked at the Perambur railroad factory just two miles from here, daily hires had even less rights than those lazy dogs that lie in front of my house."

"Those dogs are better fed than we ever were!" interrupted Mr. Rajeev, an elderly man and close neighbor of our family. He and Mr. Venugopal were contemporaries. The latter merely raised his eyebrows at the interruption and continued.

"The management and upper caste workers were always favored. The lower castes were sick and tired of being mistreated but there seemed nothing they could do about it. It enraged me, however, to see the unfairness meted out to them. They were not even supposed to use the same drinking water tumblers as the upper castes. We had steel tumblers while they used small clay pots. I decided this was intolerable. I couldn't see why we shouldn't drink the same water from the same tumbler. One morning, I walked into the factory and smashed all the clay drinking pots. As you can imagine, there was quite a ruckus and I ended up in an argument with Anamanthu, one of the high caste supervisors.

"The end result was that I punched him so hard that he lost some of his teeth. I was summoned to the office of the General Manager. He was an Englishman called Mr. Topnaught."

He chuckled and continued, "Mr. Topnaught was worried that a riot might be brewing right under his large nose. I stood before him, just out of reach of the breeze produced by the overhead fan, and listened apprehensively as Anamanthu and his coterie told their side of the story. Then I told mine.

"Mr. Topnaught decided that he was not going to get involved in caste wars. He looked blandly up at me and said we were paid according to our work and not by caste distinction. He decreed that I should pay for the medical fees and warned Anamanthu not to make an issue out of the incident. And that was all. Years later, I became the President of the Railway Workers Union, South India. Had the incident turned out differently I may have served a prison sentence."

Mr. Venugopal returned to the present. "So, Mr. Sathyamurthy, before you start talking about caste in this community, get to know your neighbors, they may save your life one day!"

Sanjeev, a young man who had had a secondary school education spoke up.

"I've read somewhere that the caste system isn't even an Indian concept, it was forced upon us by foreigners!"

"Correct," shot back Mr. Venugopal becoming professor-like, the longer he held forth on the subject.

"The truth is, the native Dravidian race is about 5,000 years old. But about 2,000 years ago, Aryan invaders from the north began making all kinds of social and racial distinctions among us, even to the point of telling us that our very salvation hinged upon what caste we were born into! I am grateful for the teachings of Mahatma Gandhi, which did away with all that. We even based our trade unions on the principles of truth and non-violence. I would go so far as to say that we were consistent with the sacred Vedic writings." Mr. Venugopal concluded with a reverent allusion to the Hindu scriptures.

Just then, Chopu and I were interrupted for the second time that morning. As we peered through the window, engrossed in the proceedings, two loud smacks resounded off our vulnerable hindquarters. We gasped and turned around to face the wrath of Mr. Vengopal's maid. Peels, seeds and our sticky hands were mute testimony to the fact that we had helped ourselves to Mr. Venugopal's fruit trees.

"You'll think twice before you steal sapotas again," she hissed.

We grimaced and gingerly rubbed our behinds, too frightened to cry and provoke more wraths.

"Now go from here, and next time don't tell lies when you enter someone's house!"

I glanced back at the window and caught the eye of Mr. Venugopal who had turned to see what the noise was about. His mouth was set sternly, yet, as I lingered for the slightest moment, I saw the ends of his thin lips turn slightly upward; then I was gone, pulled along by Chopu as though caught in the current of a swiftly moving stream.

What is so hard for men to gain as friendship true?

What is a sure defense 'gainst all that a foe can do?

The Kurral

My stinging behind reminded me that I would suffer more injury if I didn't hurry and fulfill my mother's errand. We ran to Mr. Jagan's tiny stall that served as provision shop, pharmacy, and local bar. As he dispensed fresh milk from a large aluminum can kept in a shady corner of the store, Mr. Jagan asked, "Are you girls behaving yourselves?"

"Certainly, Mr. Jagan. We're doing good deeds today!" was Chopu's rather duplicitous reply.

I paid for the warm foamy milk. It would be diluted, one part milk to four parts water, for my baby sister who was being weaned from Amma's milk.

Arriving home, I heard Amma's anxious voice. "Where have you girls been? Not talking to your sisters in the well I hope!"

"How does she know about the sisters?" I thought.

It always unnerved me to find that Amma knew more than I thought she did. Fortunately, she wasn't angry with me for being late since little Kalyani had slept the whole morning.

I realize, Mr. Crenshaw, that I cannot recall my mother ever being relaxed. I think she only rested when she was asleep. When she wasn't cooking, cleaning, washing, or seeing to us children, she wove baskets. Each basket sold for a rupee at the Perambur Palm Project where Appa worked.

As she took the milk from me, Amma said that Chopu's mother had come by the house.

"Your mother's a bundle of nerves," she told Chopu. "This evening a prospective bridegroom and his family are coming to bride-see."

This news had an electrifying effect on Chopu. "We're having a bride-seeing visit!" she whooped and ran off in a cloud of dust.

I gather that this tradition is completely alien to your Western courting traditions, Mr. Crenshaw. However, in Indian households with daughters, the 'bride-see' ceremony is anticipated with much trepidation.

The 'bride-see' event is nearly as important as the marriage ceremony itself. Without a successful bride-seeing, there is no marriage; without a marriage, there remains one more mouth to feed.

It was difficult to believe that Chopu's elder sister, Chelvi, was ready for bride-seeing! At fourteen, she seemed quite grown-up to us ten-year-olds, but she was still tiny compared to the adults.

In the early afternoon, our small house was dark and quiet. Kalyani lay sleeping peacefully on a mat in the center of the room. Baskar and Sammy were out exploring the site of the new weir. Amma took out her weaving and invited me to join her.

I took three strands of palm and automatically began weaving the material, carefully fashioning a bottom for the bowl-shaped basket.

"Amma, why do people go bride-seeing?" I asked. "Is it to see if Chelvi is pretty enough to be a bride?"

"That's one reason. But mostly it's a time when the two families meet and see if the young couple are right for one another."

"How do they know that? Do they give them an exam like at school?"

"No, Sheba," smiled my mother. "We have our own way of

telling these things."

Amma worked deftly. She didn't hurry, yet her hands moved like a machine, rhythmically intent on finishing the product. I sat in the doorway to get some fresh air.

"Chelvi will have much to do today. She'll have to clean the house and get ready. They are looking around the neighborhood for a settee to put in their house. I'm sure they'll have to visit the pawn shop to be able to afford the meal they must provide," said my mother casually.

I hesitate to say this about my own community, Mr. Crenshaw, but the level of hypocrisy involved in these charades is unbelievable. Often, both families hope to climb up the social ladder by at least a rung — at the expense of each other.

"Will Chelvi have to sing or dance?" I asked hopefully. I knew I'd be paying the Guptas a visit that night.

"No, no Sheba. Chelvi will be as quiet as a mouse. Her makeup, hairdo and sari alone will cost her family more than they have paid for cooking wood in a year," mused Amma.

"So what does she have to do?" I pestered, waiting for her to get to the fun part.

"Well, to begin with, she will bow down and touch the feet of the elders who enter her house, as a sign of respect."

I knew that this was the custom among Hindu families.

"Chelvi will also assist her mother in serving tea and refreshments to the guests. And she must be careful not to look into the eyes of the visiting family."

"Why Amma, will they beat her if she does?" The bride-seeing visit was sounding less and less like fun to me.

"No. But if she looks into the eyes of people who are her elders, she will be seen as proud. Pride is not a good trait in a girl."

"Amma, why don't we girls go on groom-seeing visits?" I protested.

"Well, we do. If the first round of bride-seeing is a success, then the girl's parents visit the proposed groom's house."

"Don't I ... I mean, doesn't the bride go as well?"

58

"Oh no!" Amma fired back. "What would you do? This is when you must depend on the wisdom of your parents. While your father talks with the groom's parents, I must watch. What am I looking for? I am looking to see if the young man is the right person for you! How does his family treat him? Is there love in their voices when they address him? How do his siblings react to him? You can be sure if he is a terror, it will show in their eyes. Your father will ask him about his schooling, work, or future plans. I will continue to watch. Sheba, we have your best interests at heart in these matters. Do not doubt the tradition of arranged marriages and bride-seeing! Now let's see what you have made. Not bad, my precious! Soon, I will show you how to make patterns in these palm baskets."

She put my small offering aside. I knew that she would disassemble it later and rebuild it into something that could be sold to the factory. She never said a word to me about this and I loved her more for it.

Voices were heard and I peeped out of the doorway. Mr. and Mrs. Rajeev, an old couple, seemed to be having an argument. From the empty washing tub carried on her head, I guessed that Mrs. Rajeev was on her way to retrieve her laundry that, by now, would be dried stiff on the stone wall that divided the village and the Koobar Canal. About three paces behind her and panting with exertion was Mr. Rajeev, accusingly pointing a pair of broken, black-rimmed glasses at her back.

"These spectacles are broken, shattered beyond repair! How am I to read my evening newspaper without glasses?" hollered Mr. Rajeev.

Without breaking stride his wife shouted, "Next time you fall asleep while reading, don't leave your glasses on the floor where they will be stepped on!"

"It would be better to live with an old donkey than to live with a woman who destroys!" he cried angrily.

"Then, by all means, get yourself a donkey!" was his wife's unrepentant reply.

Their voices faded into the distance. Mother and I grinned at the familiar scene. The old couple's arguments were commonplace and the source of much amusement.

That evening, I found I had marriage on the mind.

"Amma, do you and Appa love each other?"

My mother's eyebrows shot up. "Before we start talking about love we must prepare dinner."

"We, Amma?" I asked. "Can I help you cook?" I asked hopefully.

"If you don't start now, you'll never be ready for bride-seeing," she replied with a laugh.

As usual, Amma was preparing sambar, a concoction of curried lentils and tamarind. This, with rice or chapatthis, was our standard meal.

I scooped up two handfuls of red dhal from the tin and poured them into the black steel pot.

"How much should I take?" I asked.

"A large handful like this for each person. How many people must we feed?"

"Amma, Appa, Baskar, Jayakumar, Matthew, Sammy, Kalyani, and myself," I counted.

"Does Kalyani eat sambar yet?"

"Oh! I forgot. Only seven handfuls are needed."

As I waited for the water to boil, I asked again, "Amma, do you and Appa love each other?" I waited nervously. Was my mother going to elude my question again?

"Take a tamarind pod and put it in water to soak. By the time the dhal is cooked the tamarind will be ready to add."

I groaned inwardly but then my mother surprised me.

"What do you mean by love, Sheba?"

"I mean, do you love each other enough to be together all your life?"

"Of course," replied my mother calmly. "We were married in the church. We said our vows before God. You never go back on your vows. Here, chop the ladyfingers and watch how I season the sambar with mustard seeds. Once the mustard seeds splutter and pop, add the sambar powder."

I followed her instructions carefully but didn't lose my train of thought.

"What if you made a mistake, Amma?"

"I have been making sambar for so many years. I'm past making mistakes."

"Amma! I meant what if you and Appa getting married was a mistake. Would you have to go back to God and undo your vows?"

"You cannot undo what has been sealed eternally. That is why we value arranged marriages, Sheba. What would be the result if our children were to find their own partners? There would be marriages breaking up even before they began! Marriage is too important to rely on the judgment of inexperienced children. Family and trusted friends arrange marriages."

"But, what if they make a mistake, Amma?"

Amma sighed patiently. "Think of it this way. If we make a mistake when choosing your partner, you will have your whole family to blame. But if choose your partner and make a mistake, you will have only yourself to blame. And that is a long, lonely path to walk, my dear."

Amma turned her attention back to the sambar. "Watch the heat or we'll have sambar that tastes like charcoal."

I don't know what I learned more about that evening, marriage or cooking.

Now that I'm a mother and must think of what's best for my children, I realize that I agree with the concept of arranged marriages. At the time of Chelvi's bride-seeing, however, I was disturbed by how little control she had over her situation.

As the sambar simmered on the fire, I wondered if I would have any say in my marriage.

"Will you borrow a settee for my bride-seeing day, Amma?" I asked.

"Don't worry about these things now, Sheba," advised my mother. "At the right time, you will know everything."

"But when?" I persisted.

In an uncharacteristic display of emotion, Amma held my face in both hands.

"What can I tell you, child? Study. Do your best in school. Concentrate on that. I want you to have an education. If you are educated, anything is possible," she said with an intensity that deeply impressed me.

And yet I knew only too well, that my future hung in the balance. Sponsorship had made it possible for me to attend an English medium school instead of the local language government school. But unless I showed the potential to pass the tenth grade exams, my parents would marry me off young, in spite of sponsorship. The economic pressure of feeding so many children was beginning to tell on my father. Being the eldest and a girl, I knew that very little stood between an early marriage and me. As long as I could convince my parents that I would pass those tenth standard examinations, I was safe. But only just.

8

October 17th, 1982

Dear Sheba,

We're happy you received the gift we sent you last month. I was worried it may have got lost in the post but your letter dated August 30 just arrived, confirming that you'd received it. We're thrilled you liked the set of colored pencils and writing tablet. When you wrote about how much you enjoyed geography and map drawing, we thought these things would be useful. Perhaps, you can send us a sample of your drawing. By the sound of your letters, I can tell you are a very creative young lady.

Sheba, what does your father do at work? Have you ever accompanied him to work? Randy used to love coming along with me as I went about my work. Till I leased out the farm, he would work the land along with me. Later, he would accompany me on my building projects. I guess he picked up a lot on the job since he's a pretty clever builder himself. I doubt Randy will ever build houses for a living, but I believe it can't hurt to be as good with your hands as you are with your head. Speaking of Randy, he is doing well in the US Marines and will soon be stationed overseas.

He will be home for a short while before heading off to Beirut, the capital of a country called Lebanon. Perhaps you have heard of it, Sheba, since it's an old country, even mentioned in the Bible. Pray for Randy, Sheba. Beirut is not the most peaceful place in the world these days.

I have been reading up on India. People wise, it's the second largest country in the world! I also read that the majority of people in your land are Hindus and believe in many different gods. I know that you are from a Christian background but tell me Sheba, do you have any friends who are Hindu?

We all send our greetings Sheba, even Titus seated beside me on his old rug. He just looked up as if to say 'woof' to Sheba!

With love and affection from the Crenshaw household,

Clay and Auntie Sue Ellen

Chopu rushed in like a whirlwind. Grabbing my hand and jumping with excitement she said, "Sheba, you have to see Chelvi! She looks so beautiful! Mother took her to Perambur to have her hair styled. She's sitting straight as an arrow on the settee to keep it from getting messed up. Come, let's go sit on the settee and we'll pretend we're bride-seeing!"

Her excitement was contagious and I was ready to run out the door when Amma stopped me.

"There's no need for you girls to be underfoot there. Both of you stay here and help me make some chutney."

It was a statement and not a request and there was no way I could argue with Amma. I did whine though and Chopu supported me.

"Please Aunty, couldn't we go over for just a little while?"

"Chopu, you may go if you wish but Sheba will remain here and do her chores."

Fortunately, Appa got home early and we settled down to dinner. I wished everyone would eat faster. As soon as they finished, I rushed through my chores and sped off to Chopu's house. I reached in time to see the bride-seeing party arrive.

The Margthi family alighted from a dusty white Ambassador taxi that resembled a giant eggplant on wheels. Though they lived close by and would normally have walked or taken a bus, they chose to hire a taxi to appear wealthy.

Father and son sat in the front seat. The elder Margthi descended from his carriage with exaggerated grace, gently grooming his shiny oiled hair with both hands. He surveyed the street and assorted curious onlookers. Word had spread about Chelvi's bride-seeing.

The son leapt out of the car. He was equally groomed and wore an orange long-sleeved shirt with a green and yellow striped tie. His trousers were pleated with oversized cuffs. From the back seat emerged his mother and two other ladies. They must be his aunt and the matchmaker, I decided.

"Wait right here," the father instructed the taxi driver sternly.

Chopu's family rushed out to welcome them. With overdone politeness they ushered them into the house. The boy's family walked stiffly, like royalty entering a peasant's hovel.

A small pebble bounced off my head and I turned to see Chopu crouching beside the Ambassador's running board.

"Why are you hiding, silly? Shouldn't you be welcoming the bride-seeing party?"

"I'm supposed to stay out of the way," she giggled. "Come round to the back of the house, we'll be able to see and hear everything from there."

Chopu's house had a small loft above the main room. Taking advantage of the confusion caused by who should sit where, we darted up the small ladder into the loft and hid behind a trunk.

We looked at the scene below. Mr. Margthi, his son Prakash and the aunt were seated awkwardly on the borrowed sofa, which looked terribly out-of-place in the tiny room. Chelvi's father leaned uneasily against a little wooden table. On the low wooden bench sat Chelvi's mother and the boy's mother. A large jute bag full of rice made a comfortable seat for the matchmaker.

Just outside the door, on a wooden stool, sat Chelvi's maternal grandfather. Puffing away at his ever-present beedie, a hand-rolled cigarette, he remained silent during the visit.

Chelvi completed the ensemble, sitting trance-like in the middle of the room, legs tucked gracefully under her pink and powder blue sari. She stared impassively at the floor. The bangles and baubles adorning her made her seem so old, as if she had left behind childishness and graduated to the adult world of cares and responsibilities. To me, she looked like a lamb, acutely aware that it's intended for slaughter.

Chelvi's father began the proceedings stiffly and formally. It was obvious that this was not an arrangement between two families who had been friends for many years. With appropriate flattery in his voice, he began, "We are happy to have the Margthi family in our little house on this joyful occasion. Mr. Margthi has spoken highly of his son as a fine student..."

"He was better than a 'fine' student," butted in Mrs. Margthi.

"Prakash received a five hundred rupee scholarship for his marks in Tamil and was the highest scoring batsman for his school two years running."

"Quite right," agreed Chelvi's father hastily. "And I hear he is a good boy who works hard, does not waste his money on liquor, and has ambitions to improve himself in life. He has recently been promoted to second assistant to the daytime foreman in the leather factory. I am..."

He was interrupted this time by the blaring of horns and commotion on the street. All heads turned to see what the excitement was about and Chopu and I strained to get a glimpse. Loud voices outside soon clued us in. A fight had broken out between the taxi driver and a lorry driver.

As luck would have it, the lorry driver had chosen this day to take a short cut on a dirt lane that rarely saw traffic. He found the road blocked by the taxi and no sign of the driver who had gone for a tea break. The lorry driver leaned on his horn and the din brought the taxi driver running back. Incensed by the lorry driver's impatience, he refused to move his taxi. Everyone in the house rushed out to settle the dispute. After a verbal battle and threatening gestures, the taxi driver moved the car and the lorry driver sped past.

As soon as everyone left the room, Chopu and I rushed out of our cramped hiding place. We decided to conceal ourselves in the kitchen and listen from there.

The families trooped back in and took their places. Chelvi's father nervously cleared his throat and tried to resume his speech. "Your son is..."

"That is all very well, Mr. Gupta," boomed Mrs. Margthi, "but we are here to see if your daughter is a suitable bride for our Prakash. We have no doubt about our son's qualifications but we haven't a clue what your daughter is like. Can she cook? Can she even talk? We haven't heard a word from her since we came."

The boy's aunt took over. "Can you really expect to raise the dowry needed to marry your daughter into our family? Our boy is working and needs a scooter. She will have to be a very good housekeeper if we are to take her in with the pittance of a dowry that you are offering."

The matchmaker and the two ladies exchanged glances of approval. They were getting well warmed up.

Chopu and I exchanged glances of horror. It was obvious that things weren't going well and we disliked seeing Chelvi being humiliated, especially in her own house. Like many other fourteen-year-old girls in Indian families, Chelvi had been raised to help with the household chores and look after the younger children. She was an adept homemaker, thrifty, and a seasoned cook.

Chopu and I remained in angry silence in the kitchen. What appeared at the time to be petty meanness was, in truth, a part of the ritual negotiations. But it also allowed us all to see what kind of family the Margthis were.

The perspiration on the back of Chelvi's neck glistened in the light of the electric bulb. Sensing that things were not working out according to his plan, Chelvi's father became more nervous and obsequious. His hopes of marrying off his eldest daughter with a relatively cheap dowry were fading fast.

Serious problems arise, Mr. Crenshaw, if the dowry is inadequate. Sometimes unscrupulous in-laws hold the poor child-bride hostage. They torture her until her parents scrape together more dowry to spare their daughter further misery. In some cases, brides are even murdered for more dowries.

"Chelvi dear, why don't you serve our guests some refreshments. I'm sure the Margthis would love your delicious samosa and masala chai," suggested Mr. Gupta gently. He wiped his damp forehead with a rumpled handkerchief.

Chelvi dutifully rose from her place and joined us in the kitchen. My heart went out to Chelvi, resigned yet resolute in her acceptance of fate. I peeped at the intended groom. He appeared quite smug and terribly young. I concluded that the Margthis did not want a bride for their son but another maid for their house. The broad hint for a scooter made me stomping mad.

Chopu and I felt miserable. What started as a cheerful lark was becoming a nightmare. The bride-seeing seemed more like an auction at a cattle market. Chopu began to fidget and from her mutinous expression, I guessed she was planning something, though I couldn't see how she could help Chelvi.

Chelvi stirred the tea as if hypnotized by it.

"Sister, let me arrange the samosas on a plate," offered Chopu sweetly. Chelvi nodded. Chopu quickly arranged the triangular stuffed savory pastries in a pyramid on a plate. She scooped up the one on top and turned away.

I watched in amazement as she slit the pastry cover and stuffed in a liberal pinch of pepper powder. She placed this samosa carefully on top of the pile.

Chelvi had offered the tea around. The refreshment eased the tension in the uncomfortably quiet living room. We could hear the gratified slurps. I grabbed Chopu's arm and squealed, "You can't let Chelvi offer that samosa. You'll ruin her!"

Chopu's face spelt trouble. Defiantly turning up her button nose she said, "Chelvi's not going to offer it, I am!"

Picking up the plate she strode into the living room. Her appearance took everyone aback. This was Chelvi's show and protocol required that she alone serve and is hostess. I watched as Chopu held the plate smartly and with a pert tilt of her head announced that she wanted too wanted to play bride-seeing. She walked straight to the greasy-haired boy who looked at her disdainfully.

"Now, this one shows some manners and she can talk too! Perhaps we should wait for her to be a bride for Prakash," said the aunt smugly.

Chopu smiled confidently.

"I would like you to be the first to taste my sister's famous samosa!"

She held the plate under his nose. Putting down his tea, he surveyed the offering and shook his head. For a brief moment, Chopu lost her composure.

"Come child. I'll try some of the famous samosa," volunteered the aunt. Chopu shuffled over to her. Thankfully the aunt took one from the bottom of the pile. Chopu had no choice but to offer the plate around the room. She offered Mrs. Margthi who also took one.

"Mmmm, this is quite tasty, you should try it Prakash," she exhorted through a mouthful.

Chopu jumped back to Prakash. "Try and see..."

Without even looking at her he grabbed the topmost samosa and put the whole thing into his mouth.

My heart thumped loudly against my chest. Chopu watched him in ecstatic anticipation. Chelvi and her parents looked to see if the samosa would meet with his approval.

The boy chewed, once, twice, then stopped suddenly.

For what appeared to be an eternity, I watched his face. He looked blankly in disbelief and then his eyes got bigger and bigger. His poor face glowed and his mouth bulged as though he would burst.

And that, Mr. Crenshaw, is exactly what he did. In a thunderous explosion, he spewed out the entire samosa, showering his father and aunt with bits of potato, peas, and pastry. It was a sight I shall never forget. But instead of the laughter that Chopu had expected, hysteria ensued.

Prakash's family converged on him, shouting for water and crying out to the gods to save him. The boy was on all fours, gasping. He literally lapped up the water that Chelvi's mother rushed to him. Chelvi and her father were motionless with shock while Mr. Margthi shouted threats of court cases that would ensure the Gupta clan became the slaves of the Margthis for generations to come.

All this happened in the span of five minutes. The visitors then streamed out the door into their waiting taxi and were gone.

Can you picture the scene, Mr. Crenshaw? A crowd of curious neighbors surrounded the house. Chelvi lay in a crumpled heap in the center of the living room. I didn't know if she'd collapsed out of misery or relief. Mrs. Gupta sat silently on the jute sack holding her head in her hands.

The next second, Chopu and I were roughly dragged outside by our necks. Her father shook us and shouted, "You both are to blame for my ruin."

Suddenly Chopu's grandfather loomed behind his son-in-law. He threw his beedie to the ground and asked, "What do you intend to do? Throw them into the canal? If it were up to me, I would certainly rid us of these two trouble-makers!"

I wriggled in fright and tried to break loose. This only prompted a tighter squeeze around my thin neck.

"I will teach these girls a lesson. They think they can go about destroying other people's lives with their monkey business! To think of the money I have spent for this night!" shouted Mr. Gupta.

His eyes bulged with anger and he threw us to the ground. Rolling up his sleeves he drew his arm back and I knew we were in for a real beating.

As he was about to strike, Chopu's grandfather put his hand on the shoulder of the younger man.

"Son, it's no use bringing your blood pressure to boiling point. Let me deal with these girls. Your wife and Chelvi need your comfort."

Chopu's father breathed deeply. "Yes, father. You are quite right. But don't go easy on these wretches!"

Chopu's grandfather looked so stern. He stared at us for what seemed an age, his bushy white eyebrows accentuated by a deeply furrowed forehead.

We didn't dare move but looked on as a wheezy hissing noise came from inside the old man. I was terrified. Was the old man having some sort of attack? We had apparently ruined Chelvi's life and now it seemed as if we would be responsible for sending the old man to his grave. The hissing became a sputter and suddenly erupted into gales of wheezing laughter. The old man sat down right there in the dusty footpath and shook with uncontrolled mirth.

"Grandfather, why are you laughing?" Chopu asked gingerly, wondering if the shock had rendered the old man insane.

"I was just thinking," he gasped, trying to catch his breath, "that some day we will all have a good laugh about this. But then... " and he began to laugh again, "but then I thought, I may not live to that day so I'd better have my laugh now!"

And with that we all collapsed in laughter.

As we walked back to the house, Chopu's grandfather looked somber. Looking at us with what I believed to be mock sternness, he said, "There, we've had our little talk. I don't ever want to catch you disrupting a bride-seeing again!"

With a wink he sat down on his usual stool. Chopu and I ran off hand-in-hand to the only place where we could find comfort. Our well.

The well and the surrounding concrete pavement were bathed in a soft light from a full moon that peeked at us through the clouds. Apart from the distant voices, the only noise was that of rustling palm fronds.

"You went too far," I reproached Chopu. "You not only went too far but you nearly got us beaten by your father! You know what that would have meant? We wouldn't have been allowed to see each other, anymore!" I shook her hands angrily.

Chopu looked down but I could see the stubbornness in her heart.

Staring down at her hands, she said, "I didn't want Chelvi to marry that stuck-up pig. I did it for Chelvi." She paused and looked me in the eye. "And I would do it for you!"

"Thanks very much!" I replied stiffly. "But I don't intend to get married to a dolt like that!"

"Sheba! How can you say that? You won't choose whom you marry!"

Naively and bravely I replied, "I'm going to marry for love."

"Then you had better love a man who's willing to accept a cheap dowry!"

Please don't let this account of bride-seeing horrify you, Mr. Crenshaw. Not all bride-seeing visits turn out this way. Mine certainly didn't. I just wanted to tell you my story and this is a significant part of it.

This incident marked a passage of innocence for Chopu and myself. We had witnessed the reality of how girls grow into women in our society. The cares of this age were being carved, almost imperceptibly, upon our tender souls.

On parting that night we threw jasmine blossoms down to our twins in the well. Giggling, we wished that we might marry for love in a world without dowries.

I sometimes think about those white jasmine petals floating upon the dark surface of the water. And I yearn for those happy times with my childhood friend.

Clayton and Sue Ellen Crenshaw
63 Ash Street
Crofton, Iowa

January 23, 1983

Afternoon greetings to you, Sheba!

I hope you are well and keeping warm. Perhaps your winter is not as cold as ours. If so, count yourself fortunate! It's a quiet Sunday afternoon here at the Crenshaw home. We went to church this morning, had lunch with the Bradfords, and now Auntie Sue Ellen is taking her afternoon nap on the sofa. Old Titus is snoring at her feet. Please remember to pray for Auntie Sue Ellen. The cold weather is terrible for her health.

Outside, the ground is covered with a blanket of snow, and the only evidence of any warmth is the smoke rising out of our neighbor's chimney. I like this time of the day. It's the perfect time to catch up on my correspondence.

There's something else I like to do when it's quiet here. I work on our family history. Some folks use the word 'genealogy'. It means researching and studying the history of your ancestors. I have found some pretty interesting characters in our family tree. Great-uncle Clarence was a guitar-maker and a veteran of the Civil War - there's an odd combination! I also unearthed a fact that didn't please Auntie Sue Ellen very much. It seems that her

74

great uncle married into the James family of Independence, Missouri. That means that Auntie Sue Ellen is a distant relation of the notorious train robber, Jesse James. Well, I figure you have to take the good with the bad and if Jesse James is sitting in our family tree, we'll just have to make room for him!

Has your area been home to any famous villains, Sheba? If it has, I hope they're in the distant past! Write us when you get a chance. I sure enjoyed hearing about your school and your friend Chopu. God bless you child, we pray for you daily.

Clay and Auntie Sue Ellen Crenshaw

Sheba, Sheba! Wake up!"

Sammy tugged frantically at my arm.

"I had a dream and I have to tell somebody, now!"

It was past midnight and all I wanted was to go back to sleep.

"Tell me in the morning, Sammy!" I replied crankily.

At thirteen, I needed a lot of sleep. But it was my daily routine in the morning to ensure that the younger children were up at 6:00, dressed by 6:15, fed by 6:30, and out the door by 7:00. They had a long walk to school. I needed my sleep or I'd be a sleepwalker in the morning.

I could hear the dreary sound of rain. The lanes would be flooded and our walk to school would be a wet, muddy one. Bullfrogs chorused loudly, reveling in the puddles. "Go back to sleep," I told myself but was suddenly jerked awake by memories of a night three years ago when another brother awoke crying.

Six-year-old Matthew sat up rubbing his arm. I lit our tiny kerosene lantern and by its dim light I could see his startled expression.

"What happened?" I asked gently.

"The ants bit me," he whimpered.

By now, the whole family was awake. My parents fussed around Matthew whose cries of pain became louder and louder, till they penetrated the thin walls, and roused our neighbors. A bleary-eyed crowd gathered around our frantic family. Amma held the lantern and I searched his arm for signs of a bite or rash.

I spotted two small pinpricks on Matthew's tender brown arm. Appa rubbed his arm and hoped he would calm down and go back to sleep. But the pain intensified. We could tell he was in agony. Appa decided to rush him to hospital.

It was nearly 3 a.m. when a sleepy doctor examined Matthew who was by now unconscious. He administered an injection, which, Mr. Crenshaw, is the standard treatment here for most maladies. Whether the injection contained a cure or a placebo, we weren't to know. We were assured that Matthew would be fine and took him home.

A few hours later, Matthew's listless body turned gray. Before we could rush back to the hospital, he died in Amma's arms.

We'll never know what killed him. Perhaps it was snakebite or an allergic reaction to an insect bite. Our family that knew the sound of six playful children now had five while Amma bore her grief as only those who have lost a child can fully appreciate.

Now, many years later, I find my face wet with tears for Matthew.

I could tell by his tossing and turning that Sammy wasn't asleep. Matthew had been his big brother and though Sammy barely remembered him, his sensitive spirit often sensed the unquenched grief in our mother.

At nine, Sammy was already an enthusiastic preacher. Children gathered around him attracted by his animated style and boisterous 'hallelujahs'! Sammy had great faith in his dreams, both the nocturnal and wide-awake variety.

"Okay preacher Sam, tell me your dream," I whispered, gently pinching him. Sam needed no further encouragement.

"I dreamed of Khutar!"

"Oh no, not again!" I groaned.

The infamous bandit Khutar fascinated Sam. His exploits were told and retold by village raconteurs (with fresh embellishments on each retelling). Besides this, Sam's fertile imagination constantly invented fresh episodes.

Khutar was Perambur's version of Robin Hood. During the 1950s, he stole from the rich and distributed his booty among the poor, lower castes of the area. His thieving thus gave him an aura of nobility. In broad daylight, he would swoop down upon an unfortunate gold shop owner or pawnbroker and carry off as much as he could. Since pawnbrokers were (and still are) parasites who preyed on the poor, Khutar's exploits were lauded by the poor.

Sam began in hushed tones, " I dreamed I was Khutar. As I lay sleeping, I was awoken by the sounds of yelping dogs and lowing cattle. Alarmed, my heart beat fast and hard. I guessed that the police were here to trap me."

I listened patiently, aware that I was hearing a re-enactment of a true-life Khutar story.

Khutar sprang from his bed and burst through the thatched roof. Gasping for breath, he jumped into the darkness. He landed in the soggy marsh that adjoined his property. He ran towards a thicket of elephant grass, hoping he could hide among the long stalks. Alas, for Khutar! The thicket sheltered a bog, a muddy hole where buffaloes loved to wallow. The rains had rendered it a pool of miry clay. The famous Khutar was trapped. Flailing helplessly, he looked around as a posse of policemen closed in.

The weary and muddy Khutar was shackled to a guava tree. Summoning up his remaining dignity, he requested a bath, a cigarette, and a quick end. The bath was denied. He smoked his cigarette and was then swiftly executed. Khutar's brief spell of notoriety was over and he joined the ranks of India's infamous dead.

After Sammy had finished his thrilling narration, we lay in silence for a while. Then Sammy sighed soberly. "If only I had been able to preach to Khutar, he would have become like Paul to the Gentiles!"

🍂 10 🍂

March 3, 1983

Dear Sheba,

Greetings to you and your family from the Crenshaw household! I hope you are all well by God's grace. We're doing fine. Auntie Sue Ellen is responding nicely to her medication. She still has some pain in her legs but she manages to move around.

Early this morning, Titus and I took a long walk. We went over to the Thorntons' farm and inspected their irrigation line. The Thorntons are away on a trip (their daughter had a baby in Waterloo) and asked me to look after the farm in their absence. Can't say that I mind! You can't take the farm out of a farmer and, as I have probably said before, I hope to someday farm again.

After I returned, Auntie Sue Ellen and I went to church. We attend the First Baptist Church in Crofton. It's a small church and we all know each other and, in many ways, have grown up together. We had a missionary speaker this morning and, of all places, he and his family lived in India! He mentioned the name of the place but I couldn't catch it. It starts with 'T' and is the same area where well known missionary, Amy Carmichael, worked. He showed us quite a few slides. I noticed there are many temples around the place. The missionary said that India has many religions and that the main religion, Hinduism, has many gods. This seems strange to me since the USA is pretty much a Christian nation and we all worship one God. Not that everyone here is a true Christian but in Crofton, Iowa, at least, it's rare to come across folks of different religions.

Do you live in a Christian village, Sheba? Or do peoples of different religions co-exist? I was troubled when the missionary shared that inter-faith disputes sometimes arise and cause a lot of harm. What's it like in your village, Sheba?

Give our love to your folks and remember to pray for Auntie Sue Ellen when you get a chance.

Clay and Auntie Sue Ellen Crenshaw

Sheba Victoria
Standard 8
21 November 1983
Assignment: Faith in Our Community

I live in Maduma Nagar. According to our community president, Mr. Venugopal, there are 6,400 people who live here. There are people of different religions - Hindus, Christians, Muslims, and Sikhs. The majority is Hindu while Christians and Muslims are about equal in number. I am a Christian. My father gave me permission to interview Mr. Panikar, a priest in the Hindu temple. My friend, Malavika, came with me.

The interview took place at on November 18 at 5 p.m. My report is organized as follows:

1. What I saw

2. What I heard

3. What I admired

What I saw

Mr. Panikar's maid told us to sit on the mat under the banyan tree in the backyard of his house. She brought us two tender coconuts with long straws sticking out of the tops. We did not expect such a nice welcome. Malavika tilted her head back and held the coconut high to get the last few drops. Unfortunately, the refreshing water rushed past the straw and ran down her white school blouse.

Mr. Panikar entered at this moment. We felt shy and I think he was a bit shy too. He was an old man with short white hair. His square face was lined, especially around his eyes. He wore a white dhothi and shirt. He was barefoot and sat cross-legged, like us. Icould hear sounds from the kitchen and I think I smelled ginger frying. In the tree above, abrilliant blue kingfisher looked down at us curiously. It was quiet and peaceful under the tree.

What I heard

I took notes. Mr. Panikar's voice hardly varied in expression and reminded me of my little brother Sammy, talking in his sleep. He spoke for a long time and we were afraid to interrupt him. He spoke softly but seriously. Here are some of the things he said.

Karma

It is the most important thing to know about Hinduism. It is the universal law that no living person can escape. Our karma determines our fate. Our karma is governed by deeds in our past and present lives. When we die, we lay down our bodies like the shell of a wheat kernel, and take up a new body. But we carry our old karma into our new life.

Desire is like petrol for karma and fuels the fire of our life. If we have no desire, we can escape the effects of karma. But it is almost impossible to have no desire since even the unconscious act of breathing requires the desire to live. We make matters worse if we try to ignore or change our karma by taking our own life.

Heaven is to be free from karma and find something called moksha, which is the total release from desire. The lesson of karma (I think) is to do as many good deeds as we can so that the next life will be better. Karma is also the reason that Hindus believe in the caste system.

Vedas

These sacred books were written long ago, around 1200 B.C. by the Aryans who came to India from northern Asia. But Mr. Panikar also added that the Vedas existed even before the universe. I cannot say I understood this. All people and gods came from the Vedas which he called 'books of knowledge'. He said that there are four books.

The Vedas were written for the Brahmin priests who perform sacrifices. According to Mr. Panikar, some parts of the Vedas are hymns and mantras that they sing to the Hindu gods. The most amazing thing about the Vedas is that they have been passed down, generation to generation, by mouth. Every new generation of Brahmins learns the same teachings.

Mr. Panikar said that there is power just by speaking the words of the Vedas. This is important because the Hindus believe that God gave the words and that God lives in those words. Mr. Panikar also spoke about books called the Upanishads and the Bhagavad Gita.

The Soul

Mr. Panikar told us a lovely story. He said:

"Imagine you are sitting by a large quiet lake at night. There is no wind, no sound, only the bright reflection of the moon. You cannot see the moon since trees hide it, but its reflection is seen in the lake. As you look at the water, a bird flies overhead. You don't see the bird but you see the shadow it casts on the moonlit lake. The bird flies towards the moon and disappears."

Mr. Panikar then explained the meaning of the story. The reflection of the moon is like Brahman; we cannot see him or describe him. His presence is everywhere and there is a spark of his nature in every living thing. The bird is like atman, which is the soul. It comes silently and leaves silently, returning to Brahman from where it originated. When the atman passes from a person it gently flies to another place without a ripple on the surface of the water. He said that death is more a sleep than an end. It is like a night's sleep before the soul is reborn to new life. He said that when we sleep we don't know who we are but when we wake up, our life comes back to us and we are reborn to the new day.

This is how he explained the nature of life and death. His teaching is very different from what I have been taught. But if I'm reborn, I hope I return as a man, since men are free to choose their way in life.

What I admired

I admired Mr. Panikar; he is very peaceful and quiet. I also think he is a humble man. He is not noisy and does not make a big fuss about whether he is holy or not. I think he was happy to help two girls understand his religion. Finally, I admired the way he left us. When Mr. Panikar finished telling us his story about the lake and the moon and the bird, he looked at us both. He smiled not just with his mouth, but also with his eyes. Once he decided he had said all he wanted to say he stood up, patted us on the head and went into his house. The maid showed us out.

-The End

As children, Mr. Crenshaw, we all got along very well. We all spoke the same language, played the same games and shared similar hopes for the future. But when it came to marriage, all religions were (and still are to a large extent) expected to marry strictly within their groups.

I hope you enjoyed my paper on what I learned about Hinduism from Mr. Panikar. When we were in Standard Eight, a brilliant teacher called Mr. Thomas came up with a unique way of teaching us an important lesson on religious tolerance. Many Indians are noted for their independent, original thought which has contributed immensely to the global pool of philosophical wealth. I believe that Mr. Thomas was one such individual. Certainly he contributed to my understanding of working towards harmony in a land of stark religious differences.

As children, we were unaware of the serious difficulties that can arise when people disagree along religious lines. I recently read a quote by Jawaharlal Nehru, the first Prime Minister of India that said: The only alternative to co-existence is co-destruction.

I don't know if you've heard of the Sepoy Mutiny of 1857? We study it in Indian history. As you know, the British ruled India for many years. Once, in 1857, the Indian soldiers in the army were issued new Enfield rifles. In order to fire the weapons it was necessary to bite off the end of the bullets. Unfortunately the bullets had been lubricated with pig and cow lard. The procedure was equally offensive to Muslims and Hindus. The sepoys revolted and accused the British of attempting to defile them. Many people on both sides lost their lives.

I do have personal convictions Mr. Crenshaw. As a Christian, I believe that a person can experience harmony with oneself, family, and society when we humble ourselves under the rule and authority of God. I believe that God's rule is held together through the law of love.

Aware that our country is often threatened at the very core because of religious differences, Mr. Thomas gave his class of forty-odd students an unusual assignment. He made us pair off and only stipulated that, as far as possible, pairs should not be of the same religion. He told us that we were going to do a 'research-based' assignment. Each person had to visit his or her partner's place of worship or interview a representative of the religion. Our assignment was to be covered under three headings: 'What I saw', 'What I heard', and 'What I admired'.

Malavika and I have always been close friends even though we come from different religions. We paired up.

It's been years since we did that assignment but neither of us ever threw the papers away. I've typed them out and included them for you to read. I hope you enjoy them, Mr. Crenshaw. I've omitted the spelling errors!

Malavika Shankar
Standard 8
21 November 1983
Assignment: Faith in Our Community

I went to church with Sheba Victoria. I had never been to a church service before. It was fun because there were many children there. Many of them are sponsored but I am not. Appa says it's because I'm not a Christian but I know many Hindu children who are sponsored so I know that can't be the reason.

My report is organized as follows:

1. What I saw
2. What I heard
3. What I admired

What I saw

We all went on top of a restaurant. The church was on the terrace, which was the roof of the restaurant. There were so many people I thought the roof might fall down. A thatch covered the terrace and canvas sheets protected the walls. It was very breezy. There were lots of little children running around. I saw some people I knew from our community. A loud bell was rung and everyone became quiet. A big lady made all the children sit in front.

I didn't know where to go but the lady took my hand and made me sit down next to Sheba. The lady was the wife of the pastor. Sheba told me that later.

Pastor Stephen stood at the front of the church. He was a big man with a large stomach. He had a big, happy smile and I felt like smiling when he smiled. He spoke loudly and quickly in Tamil. I couldn't understand everything he said but the other people repeated some of the things he said. He said the word 'sthothiram' many times. Sheba told me later that 'sthothiram' means 'praise you' and you say it to God.

Some men stood beside the pastor as some songs were sung. They looked happy and closed their eyes as they sang. Some had lifted their hands together as though they were saying hello to God. They all looked so happy. Sheba's father was there too.

The men and women sat on separate sides of the church. After the songs, the pastor said something and a woman got up and stood in front of all the people. I knew who she was because she lives near my house. Her husband died last week. She's a Christian but her husband was a Hindu. She must have loved him a lot because she wept as she spoke about him. She said that she had seven children, but only four are living. Now she has to find more work to take care of her family. She ended by saying that she believed God would take care of her family.

Many people in the church cried with her including the pastor. Then everybody prayed out loud for her and she sat down again.

What I heard

It seemed to me that Pastor Stephen's speech was the most important part of the meeting so I'll write about that.

After the singing, Pastor Stephen opened a big book, the Bible. Many people had brought Bibles with them and opened them when the pastor opened his. Loudly and clearly he said that he would tell a story from the Bible. All through his speech, he walked back and forth, waving his arms about. The story he told went like this:

One day, God told a man named Jonah to talk to some bad people. Jonah didn't like those people so he sailed away on a boat that was going to another city.

A big storm arose while they were at sea. Everyone began to pray. Then they found out that Jonah had disobeyed God. They said they would have to throw him into the water so that God would not punish them all. As soon as they threw Jonah out of the boat, the water became calm. Jonah didn't drown because a big fish swallowed him. He stayed in the belly of the fish for three days but didn't die. While he was in the fish he thought about what a stubborn man he was. Then the fish spat him out onto the beach. Jonah went to the bad people and spoke God's words to them. He said that in three days God would kill them all.

The king of that city told all his people to be sorry for the bad things they had done. Everyone said sorry and hoped that God wouldn't kill them. Well, that is what happened. But when God didn't kill the people, Jonah became angry! He fought with God and said that he had known all along that God would go and be nice to these people. I felt that Jonah was so angry that there was no way he could not love people the way God loved them. There was more to the story but I did not understand it because a worm ate a tree and that made Jonah even angrier.

The point is that the pastor told everybody not to be like Jonah because Jonah hated people who did not believe in God the way he did. Pastor said that Christians are small in number and must show an example of love to all people because love is the language that everybody understands.

Then the pastor said that Jesus was like Jonah because he was dead and buried for three days and came to life. I told my father this and he said that Christians also believe in reincarnation but I don't think it's the same thing.

What I admired

I admired the woman whose husband had died. She was brave enough to get up in front of all the people and say that things would be all right for her family. I liked the pastor's smile because he made me feel like his daughter. And I liked his story even though it was not easy to understand.

July 31, 1984

Dear Sheba,

Thank you very much for your letter and the beautiful drawing. You've got so much detail into your sketch of a man sitting cross-legged under a coconut tree and weaving a palm basket. Your colorful drawing will be displayed on our refrigerator where we can see it everyday.

This letter will be a short one, as Auntie and I will be leaving for Chicago in a few hours. We're driving all the way there! It's a 500-mile journey (I'm not too familiar with the metric system but I know it's further than 600 kilometers!) It will take us a full day to drive there. We're going to a big medical center there so that Auntie can have some tests done. You know that she's always had a lot of weakness and pain in her legs. Well, of late, it's been getting hard for her to walk. It seems as if the strength in her legs is running out. Our doctor here in Sioux City has advised us to go to this medical center in Chicago to find out what the problem is.

Looks like we'll be away for a week. I wanted to send you this letter before we leave and ask for your prayers again. Adults don't usually ask children to pray for them, Sheba, but I don't mind. Be-

88

sides, you're almost a young lady now. Your fourteenth birthday's coming up in August. Will you have a big party?

Love as always,

Clay and Auntie Sue Ellen Crenshaw

irthday parties are not common among poor folk, Mr. Crenshaw. But there is one time in an Indian girl's life when a party is thrown especially for her. It's called an age-attending celebration and marks a girl's passing into puberty.

Our church frowned on this sort of celebration. For one, an age-attending ceremony meant huge expenses. It guaranteed another visit to the pawnbroker, another heavy load heaped on the mountain of debt.

Pastor Stephen was scathing on the topic of debt and its reasons.

"Why are you always running to the pawn brokers? You want to be slaves to them?" he would ask rhetorically while his congregation shifted uncomfortably.

"Your true motive is not to provide a feast for your daughter but to make a lame show of wealth that you do not have. You mock your own poverty! Weddings and funerals are occasion enough to siphon away your earnings. Let your daughters quietly come of age in modesty, as befits Christian youth!"

Pastor Stephen's sermons were straight out of the Bible and his common sense. But even so, for a girl whose life virtually revolved round her community, my imagination often got the better of me.

Chopu, Malavika, and I usually walked home from school together. As nine-year-olds, we were inseparable friends, sharing all our secrets. One evening, I left our fourth standard classroom later than the others. No, I wasn't dawdling or conscientiously finishing some schoolwork. Our class teacher who wanted to lecture me on talking less in class had kept me back.

I zoomed out to join Chopu and Malavika and was surprised to see them in a secretive huddle with Chelvi. She was whispering to them and looked tearful while Malavika and Chopu looked as if they'd heard some unbelievable news.

My heart lurched. "What happened, what happened?" I asked bounding over to them. Close up, I realized that Chelvi was tearful, but joyfully so.

"Sheba!" she exclaimed, clutching my hand. "I'm going..." she looked down and I wondered impatiently, "You're going to what?" and she said again, "I'm going to have a party. "

The sentence came out in a rush and she smiled bashfully. Chopu and Malavika began to cheer and I joined in. A party! But why, I wondered. My friends seemed so happy for Chelvi so I played along, though I felt a little foolish.

Chelvi skipped off to join her friends and we began to walk home.

"Why is Chelvi having a party?" I finally asked.

I was answered with incredulous stares and giggles.

"Why? Tell me, no?" I pleaded angrily.

Malavika spoke up. "It's her age-attending party, Sheba."

"Ohhhh," I knowingly drawled. I had heard Pastor Stephen rail against this in church.

I ventured cautiously, "What's there to celebrate?"

Chopu and Malavika dissolved in another round of giggles. I was frustrated and annoyed that they knew something I didn't. I decided not to bother with them anymore. Clutching my books to my chest, I ran home, taking the little-used footpath that ran along the public latrines.

I arrived home and found my mother placidly weaving baskets, in the shade of the doorway. She greeted me. I sat down beside her and watched her weave as though my life depended on it. Used to a volley of chatter and an animated account of my day, my mother sensed that something was wrong. Finally she put down her weaving and gave me a searching look.

"If there's any talking to be done it will have to be you, Sheba. I've been home all day and haven't enough news to fill a teaspoon."

My mother's dry humor coaxed a smile out of me.

"Amma, will I have an age-attending party?"

Amma resumed weaving. "Why do you ask?"

"Chelvi's having one. But what I really want to know is, what is an age-attending party?"

Strangely, I felt a little afraid at what her answer might be.

My mother again put down her weaving. Gently but clearly she explained the details and significance of a girl's first menstruation. "Your body will then be prepared to be a mother, Sheba," she concluded.

I was a little shocked but felt excited.

"Will I have an age-attending party, Amma?" I repeated.

"Oh Sheba!" exclaimed my mother. "Celebrate with Chelvi and we will see what happens when your time comes. Now don't think about it anymore. Enjoy the remaining years of your childhood!"

Chelvi's party was a modest affair. Wealthy people hire halls and caterers. Chelvi's family scraped together the money for a modest feast hosted for their close relatives and friends. They fussed over Chelvi, resplendent in a shimmering new red sari. But that's the irony, Mr. Crenshaw. The ceremony was just eyewash. In reality, from that moment right through her fecund years, she would be regarded as 'ritually unclean' during her menses. In some orthodox households, menstruating women are kept in a separate room for five days. They are allowed no contact with any other member of the family and their meals are sent in to them. In other households, they are not isolated but are not allowed to touch anything or enter the kitchen.

Fortunately, in the rather strict church community that I grew up in, such matters came and went with no public mention or celebration.

One more thing, Mr. Crenshaw. Every girl in a poor family knows that once she attains maturity, marriage is only a short step away.

Where there is a virtuous man, there is God.

Indian Proverb

12

I know, Mr. Crenshaw, that your country has this concept of 'dating' - a time when young people meet and form romantic relationships with members of the opposite sex. I've also heard that most dating couples eventually get married. As you know, it doesn't happen that way here. Dating is largely frowned upon and, for the most, our parents choose our life partners for us.

While I never had a boyfriend, I had friends who were boys. The distinction is marked.

Like Chopu, Javid seemed to be an ever-present figure during my childhood. I can't remember how we met. He was always there, joining in our games and story-telling sessions.

As I grew up, I realized that Javid came from an unstable family. His father had died when he was very small. To make money, his mother went to Saudi Arabia as a domestic worker. She left Javid in the care of her sister and rather notorious brother-in-law. The latter was part gangster, part eccentric and always on the verge of a momentous business deal that would move Javid and his aunt away from Maduma Nagar forever. His aunt, Mrs. Bilquis, supplemented her husband's intermittent income with fortune telling.

In truth, Javid's family was poorer than mine, if that were

possible. His mother sent an adequate amount for his food and clothing but most of this was funneled to his uncle's frequent (and failed) business schemes.

Like many of the neighborhood children, Javid had tried to register in the sponsorship program. Poor Javid. If I ever saw a person who was as deserving and needy of sponsorship it was he. However, the sponsorship program had strict guidelines about who was eligible. On interviewing the eight-year-old boy, the panel found that his mother worked in Saudi Arabia. They surmised that she must have been sending more than adequate funds for her only child. Javid was refused sponsorship.

While Javid was welcomed into most homes in the village, his family was not. In fact, they were almost ostracized. I couldn't understand why until one afternoon, my father returned home very agitated. He went straight to his mat and lay down, groaning.

We rushed to his side. "Appa, what is the matter, are you sick? Shall we visit Dr. Nagpal?" asked Baskar.

"No, a doctor cannot help me. Send for Pastor Stephen. Quickly!"

His agitation sent Baskar cycling as fast as he could to Pastor Stephen's house. He found the pastor just sitting down to lunch. Baskar's worry and incoherence startled the pastor into abandoning his meal and rushing to our home.

Seeing the pastor arrive, our neighbors converged outside the house. Was someone dying? Gravely ill? Rumors wafted around.

"What's the problem, Mohan? Has there been a riot at the factory?" guessed Pastor Stephen. It was unusual to see my normally quiet and calm father hunched up and groaning.

"Riot? I only wish it were that," he moaned. "Pastor," he said, sitting up suddenly, "I've been cursed!"

Amma started and sharply ordered us children out. We promptly rushed around to the window and peered in. Our neighbors formed a solid phalanx behind us.

"I was cycling home as usual, Pastor," began Appa.

"It's twenty kilometers each way, Pastor. I told him to take the bus but he won't part with the money," interjected my mother.

"Please woman, let me tell my story!" snapped Appa.

Composing himself, he continued. "I was nearly home when my cycle had a flat tire. I hopped off my cycle to inspect the damage. I didn't notice where I was. That was my first mistake. For I had stopped right in front of the gypsy's house. If I had known, I would have cycled on regardless of the damage to rim, tube, and tire."

"Mohan, I doubt that getting a flat tire near a gypsy's house is cause for mortal alarm," chided Pastor Stephen.

"Please listen, Pastor," pleaded Appa. "As I knelt beside my tire, I felt a touch on my shoulder. I looked up. It was the gypsy woman!"

"She touched you?" gasped both Pastor and Amma together.

"Yes! And in a very familiar manner, as though we were old friends." Appa shuddered at the memory. "I stood up. She was so close; I could smell the garlic on her breath. She smiled like a viper and said, 'Vanakkam, how is your health, Mohan?' How did she know my name? I think our children have loose tongues," growled Appa and we ducked lest he should look at us.

"I wasn't sure what to say. I replied that my health was fine and out of politeness asked if her health was fine. 'I am not worried about my health, it is yours I would be concerned about,' she said, and then she touched me, here on the shoulder."

Amma scrutinized the spot as if she expected to see a burn mark or scar.

"The gypsy invited me inside. 'I can tell you many things about yourself. There are things you would like to know? About your future perhaps?' she told me. I refused, Pastor, but she persisted. 'You know, you are not well. I know things about you Mohan.'"

"Did you go inside, Mohan?" quavered Amma.

"I would rather cut off my right arm than give her the opportunity to damn my soul with bewitching!" shouted Appa.

Pastor Stephen bowed his head thoughtfully. He looked up at Appa and smiled.

"For a man of the world, you are not very wise, my friend,"

he said.

Appa failed to understand him. "Pastor, she touched me, she may have cursed me. She may have gathered my hair from the barber to use in her sorcery. You never know what becomes of your hair with those barbers; I think they may at times sell it for a small profit ... Please Pastor, pray for me! I feel my heart is beating faster."

My father was almost incoherent with fear.

Pastor Stephen was too sensitive to laugh but his voice wobbled as if he wanted to.

"You fell for the oldest trick in the book, my friend. Every fortune-teller will tell you that your health is not as good as you think. Isn't ill health something we all secretly fear? Mrs. Bilquis knew exactly where to hit.

"Why should you feel threatened, Mohan? Do you think that our heavenly Father will let you fall into the clutches of evil because you greet a woman who thinks she can tell the future? Of course not! You are the victim of your own fear, my friend. The next time you see Mrs. Bilquis, greet her as a friend and inquire after her health. If she asks after yours say, 'God is taking care of me, thank you.' How else will people understand that God is gracious if His people lack this quality?"

Appa sagged with the release of tension. He looked ashamed. Nodding slowly he said, "You are right, Pastor. Please forgive me. I have been so foolish."

This is what I especially loved about my father, Mr. Crenshaw. His pride sometimes led him to behave foolishly but he was never too proud to repent once he realized his error.

"Forgive you?" continued Pastor. "There is nothing to forgive, but if you disturb my meal again for such a reason, it may be more difficult to forgive and even more difficult to forget!"

A loud burst of laughter reminded Pastor that he had an appreciative audience.

"Mohan, remember, where there is a virtuous man, there is God. You are a good man. Don't forget it. Take your virtue and God with you wherever you go," advised Pastor Stephen.

Like my father, many people in our community had an exaggerated fear of Javid's aunt. But many contacted her under the cover of darkness to conduct séances, tell the future, or even predict the winning numbers of the next day's lottery.

As a child, I was wary of her. By the time I was fourteen, I knew that I had nothing to fear. In fact, I secretly admired her knack of flinging social convention in the face of her neighbors. But as he grew up, Javid paid the price for the stigma attached to his foster parents.

Don't you agree, Mr. Crenshaw, that children are caste-blind and gender-blind? As kids, we ran around in a united, happy bunch. Even though Chopu had begun to attend another school from sixth standard onwards, we still managed to meet everyday either on the way to the bus stop or after school. But, as we turned fourteen, I sensed subtle shifts in the equations of our gang.

For one, Chopu was no longer an incurable tomboy. She carried herself gracefully and was beginning to pay attention to her looks. Boys seemed to want her attention and she looked at them as if they were phenomena that she had only just noticed.

Then Javid suddenly grew amazingly tall and angular. On reflection, I must admit that he was rather good-looking with dark eyes under well-pronounced eyebrows. When he smiled, there was less of the insecure child and more of a self-confident adolescent. I, on the other hand, hadn't kept up with my friends. Call me a late bloomer, but I didn't cotton on to what these changes meant or how they would affect our relationships. I did note that Appa, who had never before objected to Javid's presence, was now abrupt with him and didn't look pleased to see him at our door so often.

It did not help matters that in my naivety, I often asked Javid for help with schoolwork, giving him a reason to come home. I liked him as my friend, but romantic thoughts hadn't entered my head. They had Javid's.

Looking back, I can pinpoint the instance when my trouble with Javid began. It involved a noisy accident when two cycle rickshaws collided in front of Chopu and myself as we walked back from the bus stop after school. One was empty but the other had two passengers, a mother and daughter, who flew up and over the front wheel as both rickshaws toppled to the ground.

Both drivers disentangled themselves and immediately began to abuse each other. The passengers picked themselves up and found that they were unhurt. They too joined the fray with a litany of insults aimed at the other driver. At once, a crowd gathered and opinions flew on who was at fault and who would pay for the damage to the rickshaws.

Javid came up behind us as we watched the dispute in action. "I'll settle this," he said loftily and before our astonished eyes, he strode in between the drivers.

Stunned that a mere boy was attempting to settle the matter, the two drivers fell silent for an instant. Javid took advantage of this and set about determining who was at fault and who had had right of way. He decided that each driver should be responsible for his own damages since the lanes had blind corners and neither should have sped around them.

Impressed with his judgment, the crowd laughed and nodded. The rickshaw drivers gesticulated and muttered but there was little either could do. Shrugging off the incident, they picked up their rickshaws and wheeled them away.

Javid sauntered back to us and we applauded his mediation skills. He'd been out to impress us and had succeeded. He joined as we meandered back home. The conversation turned to school and our heavy workload. I was especially worried since I was falling behind in my assignments.

"I've been concentrating so much on my math assignment, I haven't had to time to complete my map work for geography," I fretted. "When will I find time to do everything?"

Suddenly inspiration (or so it seemed at the time) struck. "Javid, you're so gifted at art. Can't you do my maps for me?"

Javid's eyes shone as he smiled wickedly. "What will you do for me in return? After all, drawing maps is no small task. It will probably take me till the early hours of the morning to complete it."

"That's right," chimed Chopu, "And he may even weaken his eyesight, doing so much detail by the dim light of a kerosene lantern!" Chopu was quick to catch the flirtatious tone of Javid's bargaining.

I was a little flustered. "It's really not right that you should ask for something in return, Javid. After all, you are always offering to help me."

"Well, this time I require some kind of payment. Payment in kind will do!"

I did some fast thinking. "Very well," I countered, "next week at Pastor's Stephen's son's wedding, you may sit next to me when we eat. But only if Chopu and Malavika are in the same group."

I hastily added the last condition. It suddenly dawned on me that it wasn't the common to openly sit next to a boy as though we had some exclusive relationship. But the deal had been struck. And I wanted those maps badly.

ℒ 13 ℒ

October 31, 1983

Dear Sheba,

I hope you and your family are well. This is just a short letter to let you know that Randy is safe. You may recall that I said he was stationed in Beirut, Lebanon. You can imagine the terrible shock Auntie Sue Ellen and I woke to last Sunday morning (October 23) when we saw the news that a bomb had destroyed the building where Randy was stationed. More than 200 soldiers died that morning, Sheba.

Throughout the day we did not know if our precious son had survived the attack. By night, we were overjoyed to hear his voice when he called us on the telephone. Miraculously, Randy was on guard duty around the perimeter and not sleeping during the early morning attack.

I can only say, thank God for His tender mercies.

Take care dear one,

Clay and Auntie Sue Ellen Crenshaw

The day after I'd struck my deal with Javid was a Saturday and Amma let me sleep later than usual. There was no school and the house was delightfully quiet when I woke up. Privacy is a rare commodity in the slums, Mr. Crenshaw, and I basked in my brief spell of solitude. Appa had left for work. Amma had taken Kalyani and gone to visit her sister who lived two hours away. The three boys were out playing with their friends.

A gentle breeze filled the room. It was a cloudy day and the air was surprisingly dry. I could hear Sammy playing at being Khutar. The other boys were evidently the policemen closing in on him. "You'll never catch me alive!" hollered Sammy.

I giggled to myself. The younger children were so funny sometimes, I thought. I found myself dreaming of having a child of my own. Curious thoughts flitted by like 'when will I have children?' and 'who will I marry?'

It was past nine and I knew it was safer not to take a bath at the well since all the other women would be long gone. That was the price I would have to pay for getting up late.

Boys were the reason I dared not bathe at such a late hour. Amma had warned me against going to the well after 8 a.m. You see, Mr. Crenshaw, when we women bathe at the well, we wear a tubular piece of cloth sarong-style. It begins under the arms and reaches down to our shins. It is secured tightly. In this way, we are able to bathe ourselves and wash our hair quite effectively. It's the norm and no one pays the slightest bit of attention to it. Except the rowdy boys.

That's what my mother used to call the bunch of teenagers who hung around the well ostensibly to play tops or throw stones at the numerous crows. Actually they were there to tease any young girl or woman who made a late appearance at the well. They were scared of the older men but once they were off to work, there was no one to control them.

I decided that a face wash would do.

"Why do boys have to be so crude?" I wondered. "Surely Javid's not like that. He's always so polite and nice to me..." I cut short my day-dreaming and headed for the well.

The rowdy boys were already there. Fortunately another

woman and her daughter were nearby, pumping the handle of the new water pump by the side of the well. A gurgling supply of clear water splashed into their kodams.

I went to the opposite side of the rough stonewall and leaned over to grab the rope of the bucket. "Those rowdies must have inconsiderately left the bucket down the well," I grumbled mentally.

The cord was just beyond my grasp and I stepped up another rock to get closer. All at once, a searing pain shot through my right leg. I instantly forgot about the rope, the water and even the boys, unaware that a scream had escaped my mouth, startling everyone nearby.

Turning around to examine my exposed leg, I noticed blood trickling from two small puncture wounds that were already surrounded by an angry red bruise. I crouched and caught sight of the thick gray tail of a snake returning to its lair within the rocks. I looked up to find myself surrounded by four rowdies. I couldn't tell if they had come to make fun of me or help me.

"What? Scraped your toe on a rock?" demanded one belligerently.

A more perceptive boy yelled, "No, stupid! A snake has bitten her! Didn't you see it? It just crawled into the rocks there!"

Commotion ensued. I was relieved to see Baskar and his friends appear.

"What happened, Sheba? Did these boys hurt you?" he asked through clenched teeth while glaring at the rowdies.

"We didn't do anything! Your sister was bitten by a snake," shot back the defensive reply.

"Sheba!" exclaimed Baskar in horror.

"Please try and find the snake. At least we'll know if it's poisonous," I whimpered.

The boys attacked the rocks with sticks and tried to scare the snake out its lair. I think they were competing to be the first to bag the snake. I sat on a stone rocking back and forth, wailing, "Oh God, please don't let me die."

The hunted reptile finally poked its head out of a crevice and one of the boys landed a sharp blow to its head with a cane stick. The snake went quite limp. Pulling it out, the boys grabbed stones and foolishly proceeded to pulverize the snake beyond recognition.

The noise caused some of the adults from the community to come running. Mr. Babu, a gentleman known to our family, took charge.

"You stupid boys have beaten the snake beyond recognition. It could have been an eel for all we can tell," he scolded.

He was assured by one of the boys, "I know it was a cobra! Little sister will be dead in two minutes!"

"Shut up!" said their ringleader sharply. "Can't you see she's scared?"

Turning to Baskar and Mr. Babu he said, "We'd better take her to hospital since we don't know what bit her."

My heart was racing and my throat was dry. Was it shock or was it the venom coursing through my veins, I wondered. Many hands lifted me and I was deposited into a cart normally used to transport goods.

As if in a dream, I watched the faces of those running beside the cart. Baskar was petrified. He had already lost one sibling to a mysterious bite and the dread of losing another clearly showed on his face. I noticed some of the rowdies watching me expectantly. "Probably waiting to see me convulse and die in this crude ambulance," I thought ungraciously.

The small clinic at Perambur was a quiet place, owned by a retired Government hospital doctor called Dr. V. S. Nagpal. He'd furnished the waiting room with half a dozen faded green plastic chairs. Two respectable-looking persons were seated here waiting to see the doctor. And then we burst in.

"She's been bitten by a poisonous snake."

"Where's the doctor?"

"It was a cobra, I saw it."

The cries brought an extremely irate Dr. Nagpal shooting out of his office.

"Keep quiet. This is a clinic not a circus," he roared.

Baskar stepped forward timidly. "Doctor, my sister was bitten by a snake. We don't know what type it was."

"When you are bitten by a snake, always bring the rascal with you so you know what you're dealing with!" Free advice was about all that Dr. Nagpal was going to dispense.

"How long ago was she bitten?" he asked Baskar.

"About twenty minutes ago," estimated Baskar doubtfully.

"Well, she'd be dead by now if she'd been bitten by a cobra. Even so there may be venom in her and we mustn't take it lightly" said the doctor stroking his chin as though he had all the time in the world. "Well, you'll need money, of course."

Money! Mr. Babu, who worked as a road sweeper along the Perambur highway asked how much.

"She needs a serum from the General Hospital. That costs one hundred and twenty-five rupees. You'll have to take a taxi because time is running out. That costs fifty rupees. And my fee for injecting the serum is twenty five rupees."

"Two hundred rupees!" gasped Mr. Babu.

"Hurry up and decide," snapped the doctor. "I have paying patients waiting to see me."

Not once, Mr. Crenshaw, did he ask me how I felt.

It may shock you Mr. Crenshaw, but even in a life-or-death situation, it is almost impossible for poor people to come up with that kind of money. In terms of your currency, I believe two hundred rupees would amount to around four dollars. With that amount, you could feed a family here for two weeks.

Mr. Babu, the rowdies and Baskar fanned out to shops and food stalls in the market begging frantically for money. Fortunately, a kind shopkeeper who knew Pastor Stephen very well, agreed to lend us the money.

Baskar called a taxi and I was rushed to the hospital. But my misery didn't end at the hospital. Before the boys and Baskar could explain that they wanted to buy the serum for a snakebite, I was whisked away by a nurse and my clothes were exchanged for a hospital gown. I was then dumped on a trolley, hooked up to a drip, wheeled into a hallway and suddenly abandoned. For a long time, no one paid me the slightest attention. I twisted my head to look at the chart clipped to the drip stand. It read:

> *Sheba Victoria*
> *Snake bite victim*
> *Illiterate*
> *No guardian*
> *No food or water before surgery*
> *IV Drip*

Baskar was repeatedly refused permission to see me, and no one would tell him what was going on. By now, word had reached my father who rushed to the hospital. He too met with a stone wall when he tried to get information on my status.

By 5 p.m. I was wheeled into the Intensive Care Unit. I timidly asked a nurse where I was and she said unconcernedly, "ICU". I assumed it was a special ward for snakebite victims.

A noisy overhead fan whipped about the stale air in the little room. Two elderly people occupied the other beds. Perhaps, old people were especially vulnerable to snakebites, I reasoned.

And then, through the glass panels on the door, I saw the faces of Baskar, Appa and Pastor Stephen. Just the sight of them cheered me up. Pastor Stephen beamed at me, a wonderful broad beam of strength and encouragement. We tried to signal to each other, but were interrupted by a nurse who bustled up to my bed.

"Have you had any vomiting? Any bloody stools? Are you bleeding from any place in your body?" she asked in rapid-fire.

I was struck dumb. I couldn't follow her at all. My eyes strayed to the door where I could see Baskar mouthing something. Unaware of the pantomime going on behind her, the nurse became impatient with my uncooperative manner. She gave my leg a forceful slap and repeated her questions. I gulped, summoned up all my strength and almost shouted, "No!" in reply.

Unknown to me, Baskar had been mouthing, "Are you going to live?" They gasped as they saw my lips form "No" unaware that I was answering the nurse. But it turned out for the better because my anticipated demise made them determined to find a way into the ICU.

"I am a servant of God and one of my little lambs is perishing. Are you going to deny me the right to discharge my sacred duties?"

I almost cried with relief as I heard Pastor Stephen's familiar voice.

Appa and Baskar dogged his steps and were in turn dogged by a flustered nurse.

"No one enters the ICU ward except medical personnel. Not family or friends and not even servants of the Lord!" she argued.

She was fighting a losing battle and rushed off to bring reinforcements. I felt my father's calloused hand rest on my forehead. Baskar stroked my arm shyly. Pastor Stephen smiled his gentle smile and launched into prayer.

As we all chorused 'Amen', a large stranger entered the ward. He seemed more annoyed than concerned, as though his supper had been interrupted.

"What is the meaning of this?" he barked at Pastor Stephen. "Are you willing to be responsible for this child's survival? Any one of you might bring in a serious infection and endanger the lives of my patients here!"

At this point, the doctor took a surreptitious glance at my chart to determine the nature of my emergency treatment.

"Shabu has been bitten by a snake and she..." he intoned.

"Her name is Sheba," interjected Appa loudly.

The doctor continued as if he hadn't spoken. "... requires twenty-four hour observation, blood transfusion, and surgery to purge the venom."

Pastor Stephen smiled kindly at the doctor as though he had caught an errant schoolboy in a falsehood.

"Doctor, this girl has been lying in this hospital for five hours with no medical attention. I think prayer will do her more good."

As they argued, I felt a pang of compassion for my father who looked helpless and uneasy.

"Baskar, you have to get me out of here, they are going to cut me open!" I whispered frantically.

"How? No one will listen to us," he said, punching his palm with frustration. "Where are your clothes?"

"The nurse took them away, she probably has them locked up somewhere," I complained.

My brother also intuitively felt that surgery was completely unnecessary. "We'll have to smuggle you out," he said in half-jest.

"That's it Baskar!" I whispered with survival-like sharpness. "Come back tonight and bring the sari Amma bought me for next week's wedding. "Please Baskar," I pleaded forestalling his arguments, "or else I am going to become a practice patient for these knife-crazy doctors."

"I'll return at midnight," he promised before they were all shooed out of the ward.

Through the dreary waiting hours, I watched in horror as first the old woman and then the old man in the neighboring beds died, unattended. At around 11 p.m., a nurse came in, checked their pulse and then drew their sheets over their faces.

She disconnected my drip and gave me permission to go to the toilet. It was a little after midnight when I heard a noise at the door. To my surprise, I saw the ringleader of the rowdies with some of his friends. They grinned at me and began feverishly wiping the glass panels with a dirty cloth. A young nurse came out and fearfully remonstrated with them. They ignored her and made some undoubtedly rude comments, which sent her flying for help. The hallway was unattended.

Baskar shot into the ward and dumped my sari in my lap. "Hurry, we're waiting outside the main gate."

He and the boys fled and when the nurse returned with a burly ward boy, the hallway was silent and empty.

I tiptoed to the toilet and nervously tied my sari. I wasn't used to wearing one but I did what I remembered Amma doing. I drew strength from my changed appearance. Smoothing my hair as best I could, I slapped my face vigorously to get blood and color to my cheeks again.

I drew myself up and confidently walked out of the ICU. The night nurse gave me a cursory glance. Evidently she thought I must be a relative staying with a patient. After all, people who are admitted to the ICU are not dressed in saris.

Appa and Baskar were waiting just outside the main gate. The rowdies, their part done, had left. "You must be hungry," he said. "Amma is waiting at home with some food. We'd better move." Appa's eyes sparkled with satisfaction. I sat behind him on his cycle while Baskar sat on the crossbar and we made our way to the safety and comfort of home.

Clayton and Sue Ellen Crenshaw
63 Ash Street
Crofton, Iowa

❧ 14 ❧

July 4, 1984

Dear Sheba,

It is 9 a.m. and already I can tell that this day is going to be a 'scorcher'! That's American slang for very hot weather, Sheba. I'm breaking tradition today and writing to you not from my writing desk, but from under the soft green leaves of the big elm tree in the front yard. It's nice to breathe in the cool air of the morning before the heat settles on us. Titus likes it too. He's off chasing squirrels and digging up the lawn, the old rascal. I'm seated in a folding chair. The nylon braids remind me a little of what your father does with palm strands, only his work must be tighter and sturdier. I have a tall glass of lemonade placed carefully on the grass beside me. I'm balancing my writing pad on one knee. I feel like I'm in heaven. And as if this isn't good enough, I know that Auntie Sue Ellen is busy in the kitchen making chicken and dumplings and all the fixings. I'm hungry just thinking about it!

Today is a national holiday for Americans since it's our Independence Day. We simply call it the Fourth of July. Like India, we were once a British colony. I looked up my World Book Encyclopedia and I see that India became independent on August 15, 1947.

109

It's been more than 200 years since we sent the Brits packing and, of course, we're friends with them now, but we Americans sure love July 4th! It's a day for family get-togethers, parades, ripe watermelons, fireworks, beauty pageants, and corn-on-the-cob.

In about an hour, our children will arrive and this peaceful little yard will turn into a beehive of activity. We plan to drive over to Sioux City in my pick-up truck (the grandkids love to ride in the back) and watch the parade. After that, we'll head to the park to watch the competing marching bands and the big event, the beauty pageant. Auntie Sue Ellen will miss it. Not that she disapproves of these things (though I'm not sure she approves, come to think of it) but she and Tambi will return home to finish the dinner preparations.

Did I tell you that Sioux City is named after a nation of Indians? Well, the proper term is 'Native Americans' as they were here before any of the settlers from Europe. The fact that we call them 'Indians' is a direct result of the Europeans' desire to find a sea route to India. Christopher Columbus arrived in America under the misconception that he'd arrived in India. So he called the people he first met, 'Indians'.

Well, these are the thoughts that have come to me as I sit here sipping lemonade.

When do Indians get together for celebration meals, Sheba?

Love from the Crenshaws

The week following my ordeal at the hospital, my father and I drew especially close. It had shaken him to see me like that, not knowing if I would live or die. Baskar later told me that Appa was determined not to leave me at the doctor's mercy. Apparently he'd found out that the surgeons were performing non-essential surgeries on poor people who had no money or knowledge about hospital procedure. He was pleased with Baskar for helping me escape and we both basked in this rare display of affection.

The talk soon moved from my snakebite incident to something more exciting - the wedding. Pastor Stephen's son, Valar, had been studying in Australia for the past five years. Once he graduated, his parents - anxious that he would grow too attached to life in Melbourne - found him a suitable partner and asked him to return home. Within a week of his return, Valar and his future wife had their first official meeting. In this case, it was a groom-seeing visit, since the family of the bride was invited to the Pastor's house. Actually, Valar and Shanti had grown up together and Shanti was the daughter of an elder in the church.

Though I looked forward to the wedding, at the back of my mind was a nagging worry. Should I have agreed to let Javid sit next to me at the wedding feast? Should I have even let him help me do the maps in the first place? It was too late to worry. Nothing will happen I cheerfully assured myself.

The excitement was palpable in our home on the morning of the wedding. Sammy, Jayakumar, and Baskar each ironed their clothes stiff with the charcoal iron usually used for Appa's factory shirts and trousers. Their freshly oiled hair glistened in the bright sunlight. Baskar looked so good he reminded me of the film stars I'd seen on posters plastered along the walls of buildings. Amma helped me tie my sari and I was thrilled with the grown-up sensation it gave me. We took turns to peer into the tiny face mirror (the only mirror we possessed).

I was thrilled to be wearing my sari for the second time, and on an occasion that provided such a contrast to my midnight escape from the hospital ward. Appa was the first to be ready. While the rest of us bustled about, he walked up and down along the canal footpath outside our house, reciting his contribution to the wedding. As church elder and family friend, he'd been asked to pronounce a blessing upon the newly-weds during the service. Appa, who was not accustomed to public speaking, was quite nervous.

The three o'clock wedding was preceded by a parade of residents that streamed along the footpaths of Maduma Nagar, by the canal, and down the busy Perambur High Road. Though we were the same people that took this route every Sunday to church, our dressy clothes and happy faces revealed the fact that we were on our way to a wedding.

"Off to a wedding, Mohan?" called out Mr. Venugopal as we passed his house. His bald leathery pate and modest dhoti were in sharp contrast to my father's full crop of coal black hair and pressed trousers.

"Yes, Mr. Venugopal. Pastor Stephen's son is getting married today."

"Ah, the priest of the slums! That's good. It's good for young men to marry."

He smiled complacently and resumed directing his gardener on the correct way to prune a pipal tree. Hindu lore has it that the wood from the pipal tree was used to light the fire from which the gods granted humanity the gift of knowledge and wisdom. Idly, I wondered if that was why Mr. Venugopal, whom I thought to be especially knowledgeable, tended the tree with such care.

The walk to the church that day is one of my happiest childhood memories, Mr. Crenshaw. I will always treasure the peacefulness of that afternoon as our family walked together in joyous unity. I looked at each face and treasured its image in my heart.

Pastor Stephen had hired a restaurant near the church as the setting for the wedding. There was no way the invitees could have all fitted into the church. The setting was perfect. The rear of the restaurant opened into a shady garden. For the service, the guests sat under the champa trees, which exuded a heady scent.

Pastor Stephen was dressed from top to toe in white. His long-sleeved white tunic, the customary dress of pastors from his denomination in India, flowed smoothly down his rather portly midriff and stopped at his shins. Underneath his tunic he wore a shiny white silk mundu that stopped short of his bare feet. With his customary grin, Pastor strode to the center of the garden, and

112

gave a slight nod. At this signal, Mr. Prakasam began to play 'Here Comes the Bride' on a keyboard. If this surprises you Mr. Crenshaw, don't forget that Valar had had five years of western influence.

The music immediately hushed the chattering gathering. We looked expectantly at the rear of the restaurant. And then a sight I will never forget appeared. Shanti, exquisitely dressed and perfectly groomed, entered, holding onto her father's arm. She looked nothing like the Shanti I had known as a child. She seemed to me like a life-sized doll. Mr. Babu couldn't contain himself. "She looks like a queen!" he declared loudly.

At this, Shanti smiled bashfully and looked down. The women exchanged glances and the men looked away. As is usual in traditional Indian church services, the genders were segregated and sat on either side of the aisle.

The wedding ceremony was beautiful and I watched entranced as Valar and Shanti softly made their vows to each other. Even my father's blessing was perfect.

After the service, everyone rushed to the restaurant for the meal. Chopu and I found each other and giggled about nothing in particular. We were so excited by this rare social occasion. We found more of our friends and headed to the restaurant.

As young teenagers, we were still exempt from the unwritten law of segregation. We laughed and chattered together. But people watched us, waiting to spot a move or gesture that would signify the end of our innocent friendships.

Javid sat beside me as we ate. Frankly, I was more concerned about the food. Our slender finances had dipped further after my hospital episode and food wasn't plentiful at home. I blissfully tucked into my first serving of rice and curry. On my right was Chopu, pausing between mouthfuls to give an animated replay of the service.

"Sheba, eat fast, we have to leave now." Amma stood before me.

"But Valar still has to give his speech," I argued. "Must we go?"

"Don't argue. Please come," said Amma shortly and disappeared into the crowd.

I was upset. I wanted another serving of food. I wanted to hear Valar's speech. I wanted to laugh and talk with my friends. I lingered over my empty plate. Javid began to imitate Mr. Babu as he watched Shanti walk down the aisle. Javid was a hilarious mimic and I stared at him admiringly.

At that moment I was struck hard on the left side of my face. I fell off my chair, which clanged to the floor. Looking up, I first saw the shocked and embarrassed faces of those who sat near me. Then I looked to see who had hit me. It was Appa.

"Didn't Amma tell you we're leaving?" asked Appa quietly, though the violence in his voice was something new and frightening.

There must be a rational explanation for this, I thought. Perhaps Amma is feeling ill and Appa's upset. Appa grabbed my shoulder and wrenched me up. Pushing me in front of him, he hurried to the door. I twisted around and saw Baskar and Jayakumar behind us. And beyond, I saw Javid being yanked out of his seat by three men.

I didn't even realize that tears and mucus were running down my face in an ugly mess. I couldn't speak and my family was hushed and tense. It was late and rather than walk, Appa decided we would take a bus home. A bus arrived and we all boarded it.

"Why did you do that, Appa?" I shouted at him, sobbing. I was beyond caring what the other passengers might think. "What did I do that was so wicked?"

Appa stood in the isle, ironically shielding me from the other passengers. Baskar sat next to me. Amma was on the other side with Jayakumar, Sammy and Kalyani. Appa stared straight ahead and spoke through clenched teeth.

"You are never to talk or be seen with boys other than your brothers. Do you understand? You will bring disgrace on our family and our church!"

"I don't understand!" I cried stubbornly. Baskar squeezed my hand signaling that I should keep quiet. But I couldn't keep quiet and repeated angrily, "I don't understand!" Appa wouldn't look at me and gave no sign of having heard me.

Inwardly I sensed this calamity had something to do with Javid but my father's stern silence warned me against ever broaching the topic with him. It was Baskar who explained things to me that night when everyone else had fallen sleep.

"Appa was alarmed when he saw you laughing and talking with Javid," he whispered warily.

"Why? He's my friend." I could feel the tears welling up again.

"Sheba, you looked too friendly," sighed Baskar with an insight I hadn't known he possessed.

Appa had sent Amma to get me away from Javid. When that ruse failed he decided to take matters into his own hands, literally. Appa had never liked Javid's family and the thought that I might become involved with Javid, was too much for Appa to bear.

That night I woke up to the fact that I was growing up. I'd abruptly left childhood behind yet hovered uncertainly on the threshold of young adulthood. More hot tears spilled from my tired eyes and my aching head tiredly wondered, what next?

✐ 15 ✐

September 20, 1984

Dear Sheba,

N*oontime greetings from the Crenshaw household.*

Things are quiet here on the Iowa plains. We are coming into what we call our Indian summer - cool mornings, hot days, and late afternoon thunderstorms that rumble across the prairies. The storms bring relief from the heat and rain to the crops that will soon be harvested.

These hot days are tough on Auntie Sue Ellen. I hope that you will pray for Auntie, Sheba. Her multiple sclerosis has taken a turn for the worse. The disease affects a person's nervous system and the ability to walk and, in severe cases, even the ability to talk. Auntie has difficulty walking. We've bought her a second-hand wheelchair from the Salvation Army store. I've built a ramp that leads directly from the driveway up to our wooden wraparound porch. It bypasses the four wooden steps that lead up to the front door. The heat aggravates the pain in her legs and saps the strength out of the rest of her body. Don't think that I am complaining Sheba, because you will never hear Auntie complain. Some day, when you have been married for a long time like us (forty years next April!), you will understand the way old married folks think.

I have some good news and some bad news. The good news is that Randy is back in Crofton! He has finally graduated with a degree in agriculture. He will intern at the Thorntons' farm and soon, if all goes well, we will again farm my ancestral land. I can't believe it's been leased out these past twenty-three years. There's some more good news. Actually I'm not sure I should be telling you but since you're in another continent, I'll take the chance. Randy has renewed his friendship with Cindy Bliss, his high school sweetheart. I wouldn't be surprised if this friendship develops into something permanent. I guess it's best not to speculate too much on these things. One can't help but hope good things for one's children.

The bad news is that Titus is no more. The poor critter got so crippled he could hardly walk to his food bowl. When his sight began to fail, we felt the best thing would be to let him go gracefully. Charley Flowers, our trusted vet, agreed and put him to sleep. I don't know how you feel about animals in heaven, Sheba, but I do hope to see Titus up there in a friendly game of chase-the-squirrel.

Well, back to happier subjects Sheba. Judging from the photograph that accompanied your letter, you've grown into a very beautiful young lady. I'll bet your father has to chase away the boys who come calling!

As always,

With love and affection

Clay and Auntie Sue Ellen Crenshaw

Chopu's sympathy was like a balm. As we walked to the bus stop the next morning, she held my hand tightly. I told her about my late-night conversation with Baskar.

"Baskar says I must be careful now about my reputation," I told Chopu.

"Hmm, well that's one more thing we girls have to worry about," grumbled Chopu. "And here's another," she muttered as Javid appeared at the bus stop.

All at once, I felt awkward. I looked away and then, feeling guilty, I looked at him but didn't know what to say. I couldn't even greet him and I knew that we both knew our relationship had changed irrevocably. Javid had obviously decided to ignore this fact and affably asked, "How are you Sheba."

I couldn't reply. I felt overwhelmingly guilty for even being next to him and I glanced around hoping that nobody I knew was nearby. I also felt guilty for wanting him to be far away from me.

Javid's cheery demeanour dropped. It had been a mask to hide the hurt and humiliation he had received the night before. "Why won't you talk to me, Sheba, we are friends! Nothing's changed."

"I can't speak to you or see you, Javid. My father will not allow it."

"Surely you can see me after school, he will not even be aware of it."

"He will know, Javid, and I will be beaten."

If I had been slapped for having a friend, I would be thrashed for having a boyfriend.

"Sheba, you have been my best friend," said Javid and his voice broke as if he were about to cry. Strangely, this irritated me more than it moved me.

"My father is dead and my Amma is so far away I never see her. You are all I have in this life," he wheedled.

And so Javid moved from childhood playmate to unwanted suitor.

Chopu, irrepressible even in the worst of times, entered the conversation. "I'll still be your friend, Javid," she said with mock innocence.

Fortunately our bus arrived. Chopu and I jumped aboard and did not see Javid again all day.

But I was to see him every day at the bus stop for the next two months. I would turn my back on him as I saw him approaching. This didn't deter him and Chopu fielded his supplications on my behalf. He even took to writing me love poetry, which Chopu read out later with much sighing and giggling. I suppose I should have been flattered but I was not. I began to feel trapped and frustrated with his refusal to take no for an answer.

A week after the wedding debacle, three of his friends confronted me.

"Why don't you love Javid, he's a nice guy," said one.

Another reprimanded me. "Poor Javid is so alone, you were his only true friend."

I refused to answer them and felt threatened by their boldness in talking to me. To avoid them, I rushed across the highway without a thought for the traffic. Horns blared and a lorry piled high with bamboo swerved to miss me. I ducked under the awning of a bakery and looked around to find myself looking straight into Javid's face.

"I've lost my mother and father. Do I have to lose you? Why can't you love me Sheba?" he began straight away.

My heart softened. Javid seemed so vulnerable and I was sad that anyone should be downcast because of me. I said quietly, "I will be your friend Javid but nothing more. This is not the time for us." He opened his mouth and I rushed on. "Concentrate on school and get good marks. Forget this for now. I can't be deceitful with you or my father."

All at once, I felt euphoric. I knew I had said the right thing and made the right choice. My heart was no longer troubled and I crossed back to the bus stop, this time checking to see if the road was clear.

Dear Mr. Crenshaw, when you asked if my father had to chase away boys who came calling, you didn't know how close to the truth you were. And though I couldn't, at that age, confide in you, I will say now that your kind and persistent support meant so much to me.

There was still the problem of the maps to be dealt with. The morning after I'd made my sensible speech, Javid brought the maps to the bus stop. I turned away as usual and Chopu prepared to play intermediary.

"Here are your maps, Sheba, all completed," he said proudly.

"I can't take them," I said flatly. "It is better that I lose marks rather than take credit for what you've done."

"But you have to take them Sheba! I did them for you!" he pleaded. "Besides if you don't submit them, your teacher will ask why. You have no good reason and she'll give you a beating for being lazy."

He had a point. Our teachers did not tolerate unfinished assignments. I was likely to suffer a beating, this time in front of the whole class. Somehow, I just couldn't face the thought of another public humiliation.

"All right, then," I said ungraciously. "Hand the maps to Chopu and leave."

After a pause, I muttered, "And, thank you." I couldn't see his face but Chopu later told me that he had smiled when I thanked him. The maps were in a plastic packet. I went to school, opened the packet and handed them over to our teacher. I didn't want them in my possession a minute longer than necessary.

In a cool yard... the girl
With freckles
Like kino flowers,
Hair flowing as with honey,
Her skin like a young mango leaf
Tamil Poetry

16

Escaping the tiger only to find a crocodile at the water's edge. There were often times when I felt this ancient saying had been written especially for me.

I felt trapped by circumstances over which I had no control. My father was still suspicious of me and I hardly went out of the house after school. In any case, my schoolwork needed all my time so I didn't mind being housebound for a while.

The parent-teacher meeting to be held at the end of the week, had most of our class in a state of trepidation. Usually, I had no reason to be nervous about these meetings. My teachers liked me; I paid attention in class and handed in my homework on time. With the exception of maths, I did quite well in my studies.

But now I had the Javid debacle to contend with. In our small community, Mr. Crenshaw, word gets around faster than a cold germ. Our teachers concerned themselves with every aspect of our development: academic, physical, and moral. In our culture, morality is often judged by outward appearances. If a girl seems to be paying more attention to her social life she is automatically branded as someone who isn't interested in studies. Was I going to maintain my academic record or falter? I could sense my teachers' suspicions.

It was always Amma who came for these meetings. Appa's lack of education made him nervous and self-conscious in the presence of my teachers. Teachers would meet our parents alone, while we waited outside, wondering what was being discussed. If a student was called in to the parent-teacher session, it was generally an ominous sign.

Amma, who was forced by lack of money to stop studying after her father's death, loved coming to my school. She was interested in all the projects on display in the hall and listened carefully as students explained their work. She met my teachers with pleasure since she never had to worry about hearing a bad report. Mrs. Manikam, my ninth standard class-teacher called Amma in and asked me to wait outside in the corridor.

After about five minutes, Mrs. Manikam appeared at the door. "Please come in, Sheba," she said.

My stomach churned as if being put through a grinder. I entered the classroom. Amma looked equally unsure.

"Did you know that Sheba is an admirer of Tamil poetry, Mrs. Sunderraj?"

"No," replied Amma. "Why, has she written something?"

Mrs. Manikam smiled wryly. "It seems she only reads it. Let me read you something she may enjoy."

She shuffled through some papers on her desk. "Ah yes, here's a good one." And she read in an expressionless tone.

> Softly she came to me in a dream
> Like jasmine petals on a quiet lake.
> Her smile lingers over unsettled sleep, yet
> When I awake, I am disturbed.
> "Where are you my princess?"
> In the heat of the day a hen sparrow sings
> Again my thoughts are troubled,
> "Can a soul live in eternal unrest?"
> That night I wandered alone under the betel nut palms
> In the distance the jackals cried, tauntingly
> Sheba, Sheba, Sheba.

"It's an adaptation of a classical Tamil poem," remarked Mrs.

Manikam conversationally. "I have many more here. What I would like to know is this: What are they doing on the back of Sheba's geography maps?"

I tried to open my mouth but my lips seemed glued together.

"Sheba, did you write those poems? Answer the teacher," said my mother. She smiled nervously at Mrs. Manikam.

Mr. Crenshaw, I tried to think of a suitable story. Could I say I'd been duped or that I'd played a practical joke? But tears came before my words, running down my cheeks in streams of confession.

I told the truth. Every shameful bit of it. I promised them I would never again be so foolish.

Mrs. Manikam listened patiently. "Well, you had me very concerned Sheba. If you continue like this, it will be to the detriment of your studies."

I wept with shame. My mother seemed baffled as if she'd walked into a film halfway and couldn't follow the plot. I don't know how much of this story reached my father's ears, but I sensed my parents watching me worriedly. My chances of continuing my studies were increasingly weighted against me.

❧ 17 ❧

April 3, 1985

Dear Sheba,

Have you ever seen a tornado? I doubt you have because my encyclopedia says that tornadoes occur mainly in the midwestern part of the United States. A tornado, Sheba, is a powerful storm that takes the shape of a spiraling wind. It can reach speeds of over 200 miles per hour! It can throw cars and farm animals, even farm equipment and roofs of houses, hundreds of feet into the air and park them in another county. We call tornadoes 'twisters'. The reason I'm gabbling on about tornadoes is because, for the second time in my sixty-odd years, I saw one up close!

Last Tuesday, Auntie Sue Ellen and I left early in the morning for Wal-Mart in Sioux City. Wal-Mart is a real big store, (bigger than some villages, I suppose) where you can purchase just about anything you need (and many times things you don't need!). We went there to buy some fixtures for our upstairs bathroom. A pipe sprang a leak in the middle of the night, flooding the carpet of Clayton's old bedroom (which I now use as my citizen band radio room). But that's another story.

We had lunch in Sioux City at Spenser's Diner and then got ready for a leisurely drive home. As we neared Lawton, which is only 12 miles from Sioux City, the sky became very dark. By 1:30 p.m., it was as dark as night.

We knew this meant a powerful storm was brewing. I punched the accelerator of our Dodge into overdrive. As we pulled into our driveway, we looked across to Mr. Berhen's pasture and saw the long finger of a funnel cloud (that's the tornado, Sheba) touch down less than 200 yards away. Kicking up a bale of dust and dark earth, it looked like it was plowing a path straight for us. Sheba, you may not think that a sixty-seven-year-old man can move very fast but I guarantee you, I wasted no time. I scooped Auntie Sue Ellen out of her wheelchair, ran into the house and headed straight for the cellar. We huddled on the old sofa with a mattress over our heads for protection. The cellar is where Auntie Sue Ellen keeps all her canned fruits and vegetables, so we knew that even if the house fell down, we would still have plenty to eat until the rescuers came.

The whole house shook as though it was going take off into orbit. And then there was silence. The upshot of my story is that, apart from making a mess of our garden, the twister hardly did a thing to us! After touching down in Farmer Berhen's cornfield, it hopped up again and touched down briefly right between our house and garage. It sliced exactly thirteen shingles off the garage roof and took off again.

I thank the good Lord for seeing us through another near calamity. I hope you see God's hand at work in your life, Sheba. Did anything exciting happen to you today?

With love,

Clay and Auntie Sue Ellen Crenshaw

D eenakumar has just left by train with Rachel and Thomas. My husband and children are traveling to the coastal city of Visakapatanam in the neighboring state of Andhra Pradesh. They are off to visit Deena's mother who is quite ill. Or so she says. Between you and me Mr. Crenshaw, I think she will be with us for many more years.

Mrs. Samuel, my mother-in-law, was widowed six years ago. A modest insurance policy that her husband purchased a year before his death enabled her to set up a little bookshop called 'Bangles' in the central business district.

She usually falls ill in summer. That's when her friends leave town on holiday and business is dull as people stay indoors to escape the ferocious heat of the day.

Mrs. Samuel must be one of the most widely read women in India. Her shop is popular because her customers can depend on her to source almost any book or deliver opinions on the books they're thinking of buying.

But books have become her problem of late, Mr. Crenshaw. Medical books, to be precise. They're her favorite literature when business is dull or she's feeling lonely. A nervous twitch or a slight throat irritation sends her rushing to the medical book of the moment and, before long, she has convinced herself that she has a life-threatening malady.

Last summer it was severe fassitations of the lower left extremities which, she was convinced, pointed to the onset of Amytrial Lateral Sclerosis. We had to rush to the dictionary to find out what she was talking about. The year before that, she diagnosed shingles. The sores had almost circumnavigated her mid-section, she said. A feat I found unbelievable given her size, though I didn't say this in my husband's hearing.

The shingles turned out to be a severe case of scabies, brought on, no doubt, by her constant exposure to musty, dusty books (my non-medical diagnosis). Her ALS also turned out to be a false alarm. It was nothing but wobbly, weak legs unable to carry her bulk.

Each illness evaporates like the morning mist with the arrival of either of her precious sons and adored grandchildren. This year she held out for a while and then, just before my school term began, we were alerted to a new health crisis. An unsteady pulse in tandem with swelling of the ankles - could it be congestive heart failure?

Mr. Crenshaw, please don't think me unfeeling. I just can't but help see the humor in the situation. I am very fond of my mother-in-law. She supports herself, which is unusual for a woman with two sons. She hardly interferes with our lives. So when she called, I encouraged my husband to take our children and pay her a visit.

Saying good-bye is never pleasant. I feel worse when it's at a station. Harried people rushing to their carriages, hawkers, the iddly sellers who watch the crowds with vacant eyes, bring back a painful stab of collective family memories.

Deena's dark eyes and jet-black hair offset his handsome face. I was reminded again, how blessed I was to have a marriage sanctified by both love and parental guidance. As we stood together on the platform, I wanted to embrace my husband of six years, to hold him tightly, as I did with my children. But in India, public displays of affection are not appropriate.

"Mummy, we are going to go make grandmother well!" announced four-year-old Thomas. Deena decided it was time to board the train. Rachel began to look teary as he lifted the luggage in.

"Why can't you come with us, Mummy?" she asked pleadingly.

"Mummy has work to do, Rachel, we already explained that to you." replied Deena returning for her and Thomas.

It's true. There's only a week left before school reopens and I must prepare my lessons and get ready for the coming term.

"Come, let's board before we are stranded on the platform."

I gave the children a final hug. In minutes they were gone, streaming northward through the Indian darkness and out of my life for the next seven days.

I feel desolate without my husband, Mr. Crenshaw. Writing this account of my childhood has not been easy. I've laughed over pleasant episodes but wept over bitter ones. Yet, as I come to the most painful part, I'm grateful for a quiet house and solitude in which to recollect my memories.

I moved from the ninth to the tenth standard and the pressures of schoolwork seemed overwhelming. Chopu's family shifted out of Maduma Nagar and I deeply missed her comforting friendship. It didn't help that pain and rejection seemed my constant companions at home. My parents and I tiptoed around each other, no easy thing in a one-room house, and the tension was searing.

I couldn't understand why Appa chose to distance himself from me. He viewed me more as a source of worry than as a child of his. Amma chose to remain silent, but, to me, her silence signaled compliance with Appa. I can only think now, that it was the wretchedness of poverty to blame. I could go on for pages, Mr. Crenshaw, about poverty and how desperation is a state of mind for all caught in its clutches. But let my story do the explaining.

Family history is a scary thing to delve into, isn't it Mr. Crenshaw? Just as you found heroes and villains in your family tree, I find tales of heroism and foolishness nestling side by side in our family history. Some I have already shared with you, Mr. Crenshaw, but now I'd like to share two stories about my father.

The uneasiness between my parents and myself was unnerving. One evening, as Amma prepared the dinner and I sat studying by the light of the kerosene lamp, I looked up and said resolutely, "Amma, I'll study well and Appa will be proud of me."

Amma wiped her face with the edge of her pallu. Her dark eyes seemed to penetrate mine. She seemed to waver between saying something and staying silent. At last she said, "Sheba, I never wanted to tell you this but now..."

"What Amma?" I cried leaning forward.

"Seven months before you were born, Appa had some of his friends over to play cards. Appa was in a boasting mood, and started bragging about how quickly I had become pregnant after our marriage. The more he won at cards that night, the more his arrogance and obnoxious boasting increased."

At the back of my mind, I registered that Amma's voice was curiously flat, her tone monotonous.

"I sat in a corner with my head covered, quietly patching a sari. The men began to discuss how girls were nothing but a drain on a family's resources. One man said it was better for girls to be

128

stillborn; that would spare their fathers from having to labor for their dowries. Appa joined in, 'If all children were boys there would be no poverty!'"

Mr. Crenshaw, I weep now for how Amma must have felt hearing these words. And I weep because little has changed even today. Women in India hear this sort of talk all the time. But, I wonder, where would these men be if not for the women who give them life?

"Finally after a winning hand, Appa threw his cards on the table and shouted, 'My child will be a boy. I'll wager each of you hundred rupees that my firstborn will be a son.' Sheba, he wagered away my dowry, the money I'd earned through the thankless task of daily selling iddly on the railway platform."

Amma looked down at the sambar. She stirred it and threw in a couple of green chilies. Gripped by shock, my body felt like lead.

"Sheba, when you excel, Appa is proud of you. But when you let him down, he is reminded of the first time you let him down - when you were born a girl." Amma concluded with the bitter truth.

"But Amma, Appa saved my life as a baby, didn't he? Didn't he?" my voice surged with anxiety.

"Yes, that's there," agreed Amma, her face relaxed into a small smile at the memory.

Amma had told me this story countless times. It's passed into family lore and I knew it by-heart. It took place when I was just two months old.

The first warning my parents had was when the noonday sky turned as dark as night. There was heaviness in the air that seemed to press down on the small squatters' settlement. A few hours later, the wind picked up and brought with it a steady rain. By night, the wind and rain had turned into a tempest. People crouched in their flimsy homes. Amma said she held me close certain that, at any moment, the wind would send debris crashing though the fragile mud walls.

My parents thought fearfully of the nearby Koobar canal. The water would surely be rising. Would the earthen banks be able to contain the deluge? My mother rocked me and prayed, her volume rising to match the raging gale.

Black water swirled in setting their pots afloat. They jumped up and rushed out screaming. All around, people were fleeing their homes, yelling to one another over the storm's fury to run to higher ground.

Appa grabbed a length of hemp rope that he normally used to secure loads onto his bicycle. He tied one end around Amma's waist and the other end around his own. My mother held me under her sari in a futile attempt to keep me dry. The water was now waist-high.

Appa pulled us towards Mr. Golkar's house. Even today, it is the highest structure in Maduma Nagar, perched on a little mound about four meters above the confluence of the two canals. Appa turned to see how Amma was managing. Through the blinding rain, he saw her stumbling behind him, unable to balance with me in her arms. He reached out to take me. In her panic, Amma shook her head and held me closer. Appa reached out and snatched me from Amma. Holding me above his head, like a standard, he led us through the floodwaters to safety.

For obvious reasons, I loved this story. I could picture Appa holding me tight, anxious not to lose me. It made me feel special knowing that Appa had risked his life to save mine.

Then, as if to sour every hope I had, a fragment of a child-hood memory drifted into my mind. I could see Pastor Stephen and Amma recounting the story of the tempest to Baskar, Sammy and Jayakumar. I could see myself puffing up with pride as they imagined Appa holding me above the floodwaters. The story ended and amidst the laughter and excited questions from the children, Appa got up and walked towards the door. "Should have tossed her in," he muttered on his way out.

Take an excellent woman,

Even from a bad caste.

Sanskrit Proverb

18

Tenth grade wasn't all dreariness. We had our fun-filled moments and, as one of the class leaders, I was in the thick of planning and organizing extracurricular activities. One evening, after school, our sports teacher Mr. Shankar, invited four of us to tea in a nearby restaurant so that we could plan the upcoming Sports Day. We were thrilled for not only were we getting the rare chance to eat in a restaurant, but also we were getting to spend time with a favorite teacher.

Feeling very important, the four of us trooped in to the restaurant. Mr. Shankar had been delayed by some work and had asked us to go ahead. The manager evidently knew Mr. Shankar and upon hearing what our 'business' was, he seated us at a clean booth in a secluded corner. The booths were separated from each other by Formica partitions and we felt quite cozy and private.

"I hope Mr. Shankar let's us have our way this year. Last year Mrs. Sujitha was so bossy, we hardly had a say in anything!"

Paul agreed with me. "I wanted to include the lower grades in some events but she said they were too unruly. It's Sports Day, it's supposed to be unruly!"

Paul was our class spokesman and held great sway with Mr.

Shankar. We discussed our strategy for ensuring a memorable Sports Day and then Mr. Shankar arrived and we got down to planning and the more important business of eating. We relished the plates of puris and samosas that Mr. Shankar generously ordered and washed the food down with piping hot tea. The restaurant had begun to fill up and loud conversations ranged around us.

As we busily discussed our plans, I tuned in to a conversation that was taking place in the booth behind ours. I don't know why this conversation distracted me. The voices seemed strangely familiar and yet I couldn't place them.

"It's not easy living alone," sighed said the first voice.

The second voice responded sympathetically, "No, and it's bad for your health they say."

"I wish I had children at least. People are always asking me, 'How come no children, Pandian?' as if they grew in trees like tamarind pods!"

"Well, why didn't you have children?"

"When my wife died she was as barren as the day I married her. How was I to know she couldn't have children?"

"She died young, isn't it? Too bad!"

"Too bad for me, you mean. I am foreman of the factory. I make a lot of money but what's the use with no wife or children? Which young girl would want to marry a dried-up raisin of forty?"

"There's still plenty of mutton in the curry, Pandian," sniggered his companion. "In fact, I have an idea. I know someone at work who I think can help you. He has a daughter and recently dropped hints that he wants to find her a husband. Are you willing to pay?"

"What, pay for a bride? I never even visit brothels so why should I buy a wife? I have more dignity than that!"

"Calm down, Pandian, you misunderstood me. I am not suggesting that you buy a wife, but if you want a good young girl she may not come from the kind of family that can afford to pay you a dowry…" He paused to let his words sink in.

"Eh eh eh eh," chuckled Pandian as he caught the other man's

132

meaning. "Of course, if I make a poor family a cash offering, I could take my pick of the litter. Good thinking! Now I know why I made you my assistant. But don't get too wise." Their oily laughter was repulsive.

"Leave it to me, Pandian. I'll make some inquiries. We'll fix your curry before long!" Again the repulsive snickers.

"Poor girl!" I thought.

Our preparations for the fast-approaching Sports Day were well underway. We stayed after school every evening, practicing events and drills. One evening, I returned to find Baskar standing solemnly outside the door. "Appa wants to see you, he's waiting inside," he whispered tersely.

Jayakumar and Sammy were tossing their wooden tops on the hard dirt. If someone had been ill, they would not have been so carefree. I tensed like a wild animal scenting danger. What had I done now?

I hung my cloth schoolbag on a hook near the door. Appa watched me enter but did not greet me.

"Appa, you wanted to see me?" I asked timidly.

"Where were you? I have been waiting here for an hour. I should still be at the factory making money instead of sitting here like a beggar on the footpath!"

I hoped to see a trace of mirth on Appa's face. I was dismayed to see anger instead. "Sit here," he commanded pointing to spot in front him.

"Where were you?" he repeated.

"I had a class meeting to plan for Sports Day. I didn't know you were waiting for me at home or I would have come straight away! Is something wrong?" My rising voice betrayed my fear.

Amma sat in a corner rocking Kalyani. She stared at the little girl's face and wouldn't meet my eye.

Glancing out the doorway, I could see Baskar peeping in. His presence gave me a vague sense of support.

"Pay attention, Sheba." My father's hand gently but firmly guided my chin back to face him. "I told you I have something important to say. Are you ready to hear it?"

Appa stared hard at me. Was he hoping to see me looking compliant and submissive? I only looked very frightened. I hadn't a clue what he was trying to say and his seriousness was terrifying. An optimistic thought flitted by - perhaps I had received a scholarship to attend a private school for girls. The thought alighted in my mind for a second and then took flight again. Such things did happen I thought, but not to me.

"How much money do you suppose I make at the Perambur Palm Project, Sheba?" Not waiting for an answer he went on, "I'll tell you how much. I make forty rupees per working day. I am not complaining. There are many who get much less than I and have no sick leave or pension."

He paused and all at once I felt it was somehow my fault that Appa worked so hard and yet earned so little.

"We all have to work hard, Sheba, to keep our heads above the water. And there comes a time when everyone must shoulder their own responsibility in life."

My confusion was increasing. I gave Amma a furtive glance. Her face remained hidden. It was obvious no help would come from that quarter.

"Sheba, it's time you did something for the family. I am bringing home all of my hard-earned money and where does it go? Into your stomach, to buy you food, put clothes on your back and send you to school. Tell me Sheba, do you think I am getting a fair return for my labors?"

He expected an answer. I heard a high-pitched gurgling sound pierce the silent room. It came from me, from the depths of my stomach. It surfaced and exploded into a wail. I was reminded of the bells that tolled for the dead at the nearby Catholic Church and instinctively I mourned for my own departed youth and for the final severance of the relationship between my father and me.

"She doesn't know what you're talking about. Tell her what you are trying to say," said Amma from her corner.

But I knew only too well what he was trying to say. I felt betrayed by life, as though it had got tired of me and decided to cast me off. In that one instant, Mr. Crenshaw, all of my dreams evaporated like puddles of water on a hot April day.

My father leaned forward and grabbed my shoulders. Shaking me he shouted, "Sheba, you are a good student but nothing out of the ordinary. What will you achieve once you finish your studies? I can't afford to let you continue a pursuit that will benefit neither you nor your family. And I cannot afford to feed and clothe you forever."

Here he paused and looked out the doorway toward his eldest son.

"Baskar has shown much more promise as a student. He will go to college, get a good job, and help support this household."

My sobs quieted. I was puzzled. From where was Appa going to get the money to send Baskar to college?

"Sheba, there is a good man at the project; he is a foreman and a good Christian. His name is Pandian and I have already arranged for him and his mother to see you. You wouldn't have realized it, but he told me he saw you last Sunday, at church as a matter of fact." Appa gave an awkward laugh as though I should be humored by this fact.

I froze as Appa's low laugh sparked a memory. "Oh God, no! Pandian. He was the one I heard talking in the hotel last week!" I thought. His assistant had been referring to me. I felt violated, as if I'd been raped without having been touched. That stupid assistant had concocted this whole scheme to ruin my life. I was furious with a man I'd never met and never wanted to meet.

"Sheba," Amma continued softly, "you know we cannot afford a dowry. The man is a friend and fellow worker of your father's. He is from a good family. Besides we are poor and should be thankful for what comes our way."

Appa got up as if impatient with all this talk. "You will meet me at the church tomorrow directly after school, Sheba. I have already arranged for an informal visit." He paused as my head remained bowed. "You should be happy! Many girls don't get the chance to talk with their husbands before the wedding. I am giving you the chance to have a conversation with your future husband." Appa's attempts to jolly me along enraged me.

I shook my head angrily, like a horse ridding itself of flies.

"I don't want to marry, Appa! Not now, not like this. I'm not ready!" The words sputtered from my mouth. Like a cornered mongoose, I was determined to put up a brave fight.

But Appa, the predator, had the advantage. His back was not up against the wall. Mine was. He repeated his ultimatum. "You will be at the church tomorrow at 4 p.m. You will meet Mr. Pandian whom your mother and I have chosen for you. And you will marry him. I have wasted enough time here already, you have received more than you deserve!" My father turned away sharply. The house was silent for a moment. Appa had laid down the law and I would have to abide by it. But the bitter sense of betrayal made me rebellious.

"I know who you're talking about, he's old and a widower. How could you do this to me Appa?" I lost control as my emotions got the better of me. Tears and spittle spewed as I flung my accusation at him.

"Tell me Appa, how much?"

Appa looked at me blankly. Then shock registered on his face. I don't know which shocked him more, the fact that I knew I'd been sold, or my boldness in asking.

I pleaded once more, "How much are you selling me for? I just want to know what your eldest daughter is worth to you!"

Appa took a step towards me and I thought he would hit me. Then he stopped mid-stride and grimaced. He shook a finger in my face. "Just be there tomorrow," he snarled. Throwing up his hands in exasperation, he spun around and stormed out the door.

"It isn't fair, it just isn't fair!" The mantra encircled my mind like a cruel spider web. I made for the door and Amma made no move to stop me. Baskar tried to catch me as I stumbled past him. My younger brother always seemed so much wiser than his age.

"What are you doing, Sheba? Where are you going?"

"I don't know, just out, I have to get away from this house!" was all I could say through my tears.

"Sheba, Appa is just worried about money right now. Don't be upset. Don't worry about it. We'll think of a way out."

I wished my gentle brother could so easily right the wrongs in my life. But I knew there was nothing he could do and shaking my arm free I ran.

As I ran, the pounding in my head kept beating out the rhythm, "It isn't fair. It isn't fair." I headed for the well, my childhood refuge in times of trouble. Unfortunately Mrs. Jyothimani was already there and in animated discussion with an old man whom I did not recognize. I was in no mood to endure her and her peeves. I turned left down a narrow, poorly lit footpath.

I wandered along, not really seeing where I was going. I blamed everybody and everything about my predicament. I blamed God for not saving me from a teenage marriage. I blamed Amma for not standing up to Appa in what she surely knew was a gross injustice. I even blamed you, Mr. Crenshaw. If you hadn't sponsored me in the first place, I would never have had any hopes of getting an education. I would never have known that I could make something out of my life by studying.

A sharp pain tore through my foot and shook me out of my self-pity. I had stubbed my big toe on an angular rock. The nail had almost been torn off. I had no choice but to walk on and blood dripped a crimson trail on the dirt path.

Turning the corner, I found myself on Mr. Venugopal's lane. I walked towards his house not really knowing why. As I neared, I saw some of his household help engaged in the bizarre act of lifting the carcass of a large dog. I stared in disbelief.

"A passing truck hit it this afternoon. The poor creature was flung over the low wall and landed in our courtyard." The voice of Mrs. Venugopal, a venerable old lady whom I respected very much, broke into my thoughts. I was a little embarrassed at being caught staring. Like her husband, Mrs. Venugopal was concerned with the happenings in our growing community and could always be counted on for the latest Maduma Nagar news.

"Where are you off to, Sheba?" She inquired kindly.

"Oh ... uh... " I gave a weak laugh and desperately tried to think of an answer. "I'm going to purchase some lentils for our evening supper."

Actually that was what I'd planned to say.

Instead I blurted out, "It's not fair!"

"Oh my! What's not fair, child?"

I shook my head. I wanted to move on before I burst into tears but I winced as I took a step forward. I'd forgotten about my bleeding toe.

"Child, you're bleeding!" said Mrs. Venugopal with a horrified glance at my foot. "Come in and we'll put some medicine on that wound."

She bustled in and called out to a maid to bring some water. I was directed to a bench on the verandah.

Mr. Venugopal came out to see what the commotion was about.

"Oh my goodness!" he exclaimed looking at my bleeding toe. "Don't cry! Auntie will make it better. What is about today, Ma? he asked Mrs. Venugopal. "First that old cur was hit clean into our compound. I've never seen anything like it in my life! Now young Sheba arrives bleeding on our doorstep. It reminds of 1948 when ..."

"She said 'It isn't fair', Pa." His wife interrupted him, in a kind attempt to bring his attention back to me.

"Well of course it isn't fair! When dogs and girls start falling into your home out of the blue, I certainly don't think it's fair at all." Mr. Venugopal chuckled pleased with his humor.

"Will she need stitches, Ma?" asked one of the young maids who was gently cleaning my toe with a piece of fine muslin.

"No need. Just find me a plaster and we will have it in fine shape," was Mrs. Venugopal's reassuring reply. Kindness from such unexpected quarters, at a time when I hungered for a kind word, had me in tears again. The perceptive Mrs. Venugopal understood. "What's happened, Sheba? Why are you crying?"

"Her foot must be hurting badly," said the old man with the air of seasoned doctor.

"Shush! Let the child speak. Sheba, what's the matter?"

My shoulders sagged. My hands dangled limply between my knees. I breathed deeply and said, "Appa said I have to get married.

A man is coming to see me at church tomorrow afternoon. It's not fair!" I began to sob again.

The old couple looked at me thoughtfully. I knew they understood all too well what I was going through. After a short pause, Mr. Venugopal ventured some sage counsel.

"A lotus rising from the mud."

I hiccupped blankly.

"That's right. You are a lovely lotus blossom rising from the miry clay. Right now, everything around you seems dirty and rotten but you will come to see the beauty of this."

His metaphor had me stumped and I evidently looked as blank as I felt.

"Well Sheba, girls get married. It is the way of our society. Do you want to remain single all your life?" Mr. Venugopal looked so comical in his earnestness to give me good advice. His arched eyebrows nearly touched his baldpate. Mrs. Venugopal gave me a wry look and nudged the old man's arm. "Pa, can you please ask the maids to make some coffee?"

"Praise food digested, a wife whose youth has departed and the grain which has come into the house." His eyes twinkled. "So say the sages and therefore I will never cease to sing your praises, wife." Having delivered this cryptic speech, he shuffled off inside.

Mrs. Venugopal sat down next to me. Her gentle demeanor made me feel that I wasn't so alone after all. When I think back to that awful day, I thank God for the kind Hindu woman who comforted me in my darkest hour.

I poured out my heart. My family was poor and I was a girl. My redeeming value lay outside the home and so my father was 'selling' me to a co-worker.

That just about summed it up. It was bad luck that I would have to leave school at such an early age. Of course, I didn't really believe in 'luck'. But in my grief, I felt it easier to name luck as the villain rather than God whom I'd always considered caring and who, I felt even then, had a plan for my life.

Two tumblers of comforting creamy brown coffee arrived.

"Tell me Sheba, what does your Book say about parents?"

"It says we should honor our mothers and fathers," I mumbled and took a sip of the hot coffee. Its warmth revived me. I looked at Mrs. Venugopal suspiciously. Was she going to force me to obey my parents?

"Have you done that all your life?"

"Of course, Mrs. Venugopal," I replied honestly.

"How, Sheba? How do you honor your mother and father?"

"Well," I faltered, "I suppose by doing what they wish me to do." I continued hurriedly, "But, Mrs. Venugopal, they are of a different age. They seem to fear that as a girl I will never amount to anything, with or without an education!"

"So then, even in their fear they ultimately want what is best for you. On the one hand, you could accept your father's demand. I am afraid it is not the life you envisioned for yourself but, strictly speaking, it is the way of obedience. On the other hand ..."

"I could refuse to meet that old ... er ... that old Mr. Pandian and his mother. In reality I would be honoring my father even more because I will do what he himself believes is impossible. I will work for my education and I will fulfill my dream!" I finished excitedly.

"You will be able to help your family far better if you are educated rather than if you are ignorant and perpetually pregnant," said Mrs. Venugopal in her soft, reassuring voice.

"Even so," she went on, "your father will not take your disobedience lightly."

"But Mrs. Venugopal, I am his daughter and I hardly think he will kill me! After all, he had better understand that I am nearly an adult. If I am ready for marriage, surely I am capable of making this decision."

Mr. Crenshaw, I have always been an idealist. Perhaps, that's why my battles have been that much tougher. I believed it then and I believe it now: If one has pure motives everything must work out. All my life I had been conditioned to obey and honor every word from my parents and elders. Now my heart was telling me that obedience might mean something more complicated than a simple yes or no.

140

I went home feeling relieved. Amma and the younger children were lying down on the mat. Amma looked up when I entered and then wordlessly lay down again. I knew that she was glad to see me back. Appa still hadn't returned. Baskar sat studying by the light of a small kerosene lamp. Taking my math book out, I sat next to him. We exchanged smiles and continued our studies together as though no power on earth could come between our books and us.

In a hundred, one hero is found;

In a thousand, one wise.

Indian Proverb

❧ 19 ❧

awn comes early on India's eastern coast. I rose and went about my morning chores. The heavy morning air carried the scent of wood fires. The rooster's wake-up call, infants wailing for their first meal of the day, the hacking of kindling for smoky fires and the rumble of lorries from the Perambur-Madras highway - these familiar noises were a part of my consciousness.

My walk to the bus stop was uneventful. I greeted Mr. Jagan as I passed his small shop. Sammy forcefully defended his favorite cricket player against Jayakumar's slurs and Baskar explained why India had beaten Australia in the most recent one-day test match. My thoughts were on the day ahead. As we passed by Mrs. Venugopal's house, I peeked in. The old lady saw me from the verandah and called out, "How's your foot?"

"Better, thank you," I answered feeling a little shy.

"You're a brave girl, Sheba," she said with a satisfied nod.

I was encouraged because brave was not how I felt just then. I was aware that the day would mark a significant transition in my life. Childhood is truly short in India and I keenly longed for a time when life seemed so much simpler.

I wished that my dilemma was like a math problem where I could work backwards and find a solution. I thought about my life running backwards. A widow at forty, grandmother at thirty-five, four children by twenty, and married at fifteen. The equation added up to bleakness and again my mind began to spiral towards despair.

Once at school, I tried to force my problem to the back of my mind and concentrate on lessons and the people around me.

My memories are so fresh, Mr. Crenshaw. I can effortlessly conjure up the way I felt that day and maybe it's because I teach in the same school where I struggled so hard. The classroom was then as it is now. A dark room with a high ceiling. Two large fans drone overhead to keep the air and flies moving. The shuttered windows remain open except during the monsoon gales. Sunlight filters in to supplement the glow cast by the naked light bulbs suspended from the ceiling.

I recall shifting uncomfortably on the wooden chair, trying to grapple with the math problem chalked on the blackboard. I needed all my powers of concentration but was distracted by a bothersome fruit fly intent on tickling my sweat-streaked neck.

"You have twenty minutes to solve this problem. There will be no quiz this Friday, so this test will be counted along with your final exam marks. I don't want anyone whispering or exchanging glances." Mr. Bhagyaraj glared at the forty-nine students in front of him.

I couldn't study math at the best of times and late afternoon seemed the worst of times. I was scared of Mr. Bhagyaraj. Young and new to the teaching profession, his temperament hardened as his confidence sagged.

Would you believe that I can still see the problem as it was written in his nearly illegible cursive covering the large blackboard? It went something like this:

Javid gave Sastri 1/2 of his mystery books.

Sastri gave Krishnan 1/2 of the books he got from Javid.

Krishnan gave Naib 1/2 of the books he got from Sastri.

Naib only got four books.

How many books did Sastri start with?

My problem, Mr. Crenshaw, was that I saw mathematics as one big problem and not as an opportunity to learn. I slouched in my chair, my spine arched uncomfortably against the wooden slat that served as a backrest, and decided to daydream. The twenty minutes began to tick away. I wasted precious time, unable even to think of something to daydream about.

The bothersome fly landed on my neck. Sensing my opportunity to finish off the little pest, I swatted it aggressively. To my horror, my pencil slid from my clammy grip and flew through the air to strike Mr. Bhagyaraj on the leg as he walked past my workbench. Forty-nine eyes looked up as the teacher exclaimed, "Ah!" He looked at me incredulously, as though the projectile was a preemptive attack. I grinned sheepishly and said a meek "sorry."

"I am not seeing the humor in this, Sheba! If you think your marks in Mathematics are good enough for you to play games with your teacher then you are sadly mistaken!"

He gave me a painful pinch on the back of my arm to show he meant business. I retrieved my pencil. If only math was easier, I wished sadly.

In India, attending school is one thing. Learning is another. Often, lessons are handed out and examinations are handed in while little classroom instruction is accomplished. This is especially true when the teacher is weak. Looking back, I suspect this was the case with Mr. Bhagyaraj. But what could I do? I had to pass in all my subjects or I would not qualify for higher education.

I knew I needed tutoring in math. But my family couldn't (and wouldn't under the present circumstances) pay for extra tuition. I needed someone who could identify the areas of my weaknesses and help me think positively about those problems. Sometimes the answer is simple when you work backwards, which is how I learned to solve the problem above and, as you have probably done so by now, found the answer to be thirty-two.

I walked slowly to the bus stop after school. Lorries, cars, rickshaws, and bicycles spilled onto the footpath. Pedestrians maneuvered between traffic and shops that spilled on to the street in a riot of awnings and wares. I automatically navigated my way through the chaos, still smarting from the pinch I'd received in math class. I was forced to stop in front of a shop selling copper pots while a large truck clumsily tried to reverse out of a tiny parking spot on to the busy street.

In the din of horns and shouts from well-meaning passers-by trying to guide the lorry out, I stood looking blankly across the street. There, amid the dust and hustle of the busy market was Chopu. "Chopu!" I yelled excitedly. I hadn't seen Chopu for almost a year. I felt happy just seeing her pert, cheeky face. Wherever Chopu was, adventure was never far behind. She turned and saw me. "Sheba!" she whooped.

Weaving her way through the perilous traffic, she rushed over and we hugged each other joyfully. Before I could say anything, she began talking as we walked down the road.

"Sheba, you will never guess who I saw this morning!" Not waiting for a reply, she continued, "I saw Mrs. Margthi at the market! You remember, Prakash's mother! At first, I just watched her as she haggled over the price of ladyfingers. Then she turned and looked me straight in the eye. She must have some sixth sense because I was only looking at her and hadn't said a word. I thought she wouldn't recognize me, but she knew who I was. She looked at me with such a stern look, I'm sure she was casting the evil eye."

"Oh really, Chopu!" I countered, surprised that she had still hadn't lost her childish sense of intrigue. "You have such an imagination! I'm sure she wouldn't waste her 'evil eye' on you!"

"No Sheba, she glared at me as if I was the cause of some great calamity that had befallen her."

"It's no wonder Chopu. Hadn't you heard that Prakash joined the Army? He's serving on the India-Pakistan border. I hear he's a cook. I hope he's a better cook than he was a prospective groom. Maybe he's learned the secret of making good samosas!"

"Maybe he uses my special recipe for his commanding officers," hooted Chopu.

We stopped in our tracks and doubled up with laughter at the memory of Chelvi's disastrous first bride-seeing. Chelvi went on to marry the second man who came to see her and I can assure you, Mr. Crenshaw, that Chopu and I weren't allowed anywhere near the house on that particular bride-seeing visit.

I looked carefully at my friend. I found it odd that she wasn't carrying a school bag. I took her hands in mine and looked searchingly into her eyes with that familiarity that only old friends can achieve. "How is your family, Chopu? I heard from Dhanam awhile ago that your father is sick."

Chopu's smile faded when I mentioned her father. We had stopped outside a rice merchant's shop and she suddenly became intensely interest in a sack of broken rice filled to the brim. She absentmindedly splayed her fingers through the silky rice.

"Are you girls here to buy or to gossip?" asked the shopkeeper had noticed Chopu's hand in the rice sack.

"No, uncle we are just deciding what grain to buy for my sick mother at home," shot back Chopu, her brown eyes large and innocent.

"Decide and pay for it. Or move along," was the curt rejoinder.

Hand-in-hand we walked down the road until we came to a narrow gap between two buildings. We stepped inside the narrow shaded alley. A couple of pigeons cooed sadly from a ledge.

"Yes, my father is sick but he has his provident fund which provides for us. Besides, his factory is paying us his full salary until he recovers. I am going to college, Sheba, imagine that!" chirped Chopu.

I looked at my friend dubiously. I knew her too well to believe her overly optimistic story.

"Your father's company doesn't pay provident fund to daily laborers, and if you are studying, where are your books, Chopu?"

With anybody else, Chopu would have blindly continued with her lame story but we knew each other too well. We stood there in silence for a very long time, Mr. Crenshaw. I was beginning to wonder if I had transgressed the boundaries of familiarity. Chopu's sniffling broke the silence. The sniffles soon developed into a torrent of tears. My heart broke. It was so rare to see Chopu cry. Haltingly, between sobs, she told me that her father had been incapacitated by a massive stroke.

"But now he's not sick at all," she sobbed. "He's dead, Sheba."

I felt her pain, Mr. Crenshaw. Unlike my father and I, Chopu and her father had always been extremely close. Her mischievous ways exasperated him sometimes but she always managed to make him laugh away his anger. He called her his "Appa ponnu" which means 'Daddy's girl'.

It turned out that her father had died a week before. His company had paid them five thousand rupees in sympathy. But it did not serve the living, only the dead. In other words, five thousand rupees was only enough to give the poor man a decent funeral.

"After the cremation ceremony, my mother, grandfather and I sat at home in the dark for two days. We were without hope until my father's foreman came to our house and offered me the same job that my father had held." Chopu broke down again and her words were nearly indecipherable from her sobs.

"Sheba ... I ... don't ... know ... what ... to do!"

Chopu choked on a sob and looked directly into my face. Her eyes were great swollen reservoirs of tears. Broken yet defiant, she reminded me of an ant daring to raise its tiny fists to the heavens in protest against a flood that threatened to sweep away it and its own.

"What are you going to do?" I asked helplessly.

"I have one hope, Sheba," she said scrubbing her face dry. "If I pass my exams with eighty per cent I can apply for a scholarship that will keep me in school and allow me to bring home enough money for us to live on, at least until my mother can find work."

"Is that possible, Chopu? How are your marks right now?" I asked sympathetically.

"I am behind, Sheba. " Resignation and fear crept into her voice. She checked herself. "If only I had a tutor I could easily catch up. What to do, Sheba?"

I thought long and hard as the pigeons cooed mournfully above us. I wanted to blurt out my own horrible news but I couldn't bring myself to do it. Actually, the more I focused on Chopu and her problems, the stronger I felt, as though my own precarious situation diminished in size next to hers.

As I stood there thinking, the most amazing thing happened.

Words came into my mind like gentle feathers falling from the pigeons above.

"From everyone who has been given much..."

But what could I give? I had no money and certainly no connections at the factory...

"Much has been demanded..."

What could be demanded of me? And then an idea popped into my head. Just like that. Effortlessly.

"Chopu, how are you in math?

"Math is easy. The least of my problems," she said carelessly.

"Wonderful!" I cheered and jumped high into the air. My school bag fell off my shoulder and landed with a thud that sent the pigeons scurrying in a soft swoosh of feathers and dust.

Chopu stared at me bewildered. Before I could explain the reason for my elation, a small cameo being enacted at the end of the alley caught my attention. An old lady stepped into the alley. She put out her hands and a pair of childish hands hooked up with hers. She pulled but obviously whoever was around the corner, resisted. She pulled again and looked coaxingly at the unseen figure which, though it held her hands tightly, refused to emerge from around the corner. Suddenly I wondered if I wasn't like that unseen figure. Was I resisting the direction that God wanted for me? Should I struggle, or was there really a God directing me?

And there and then, my faith soared. I knew that God was in control. And I knew what I had to do.

"Chopu, you and I are going to help each other. I'll tutor you in your weak subjects and you tutor me in math."

The look on Chopu's face, the look of someone who had found hope again, made me laugh with delight. I was reminded of how precious a friend she'd been. The truth is, Mr. Crenshaw, I had always felt slightly guilty that I was a sponsored child while Chopu was not. Her exclusion from what, at times, was perceived as an elite club of opportunity hurt me deeply. I even brought her once to the weekly activity for sponsored children held in Pastor Stephen's rooftop church. I was sternly warned that I should not try and play program director henceforth and Chopu was not allowed to come back.

As Chopu and I parted that evening, I knew that it was the first time I had ever truly cared enough to help someone come through something that could have destroyed them. I looked forward to renewing our friendship. But as I watched her retreating figure, I was reminded that I had other problems to deal with that evening.

Like a lily among thorns
Is my darling among the maidens?

Song of Solomon 2:1

❦ 20 ❦

Four 'o'clock was fifteen minutes away and I had no idea what I was going to do. I kept seeing my life from the perspective of a tragic story. Sheba marries at fifteen, Sheba is pregnant at fifteen and Sheba's life is over at fifteen.

I didn't understand why I had to meet my father and Mr. Pandian. I didn't have to be shown to the man; he had already seen me and decided I was good childbearing material.

I wandered down the busy Perambur highway. In a dream, I watched myself approach the narrow stairway that led up to the rooftop church. And then I passed by it and kept going, drifting past familiar shops. I peeked into the teashop - the clock on the wall announced that seventeen minutes had passed by since four o'clock.

I crossed the busy highway and strolled down a lane that looked inviting because it was lonely and the solitude promised peace of mind. I walked till the lane unexpectedly swelled with people and animals. I passed under shop awnings, miraculously dodged cattle, cars, people and possessions. And as I walked, my mind a blank, I felt as though I were being cleansed from the trauma that I had endured the day before. I walked for hours and unknowingly, but perhaps instinctively, I found myself back at the church.

Though it was late I could see the glow of a kerosene lantern, its red beams escaping through chinks in the thatch. Climbing the stairs I realized that Pastor Stephen was the man I should have gone to in the first place. My fear and sense of disgrace had kept me away.

I ducked under the low doorway and sat down on a mat near the pastor's small desk. This little room, crudely partitioned from the main church hall, was his study, counseling room and prayer chamber. He did not look up but I knew that he knew I was there. We remained silent for while. And then my tears began again, the familiar salty taste dripping past my lips.

I don't know why I cried, Mr. Crenshaw. Was it the pain of my disobedience or just weariness? Pastor Stephen left his desk and sat cross-legged beside me. We must have looked like two disciples deep in silent prayer.

I heard a sound and looked up. My pastor and lifelong spiritual mentor were weeping with - and for - me. Wordlessly he identified with my deepest pain. Words could never have said so much. In a torrent of pent-up rejection and hurt I sobbed, "Why does my father hate me so much, Pastor Stephen?"

"Hate you? Your father loves you, Sheba."

"If he loves me so much, why does he intend to sell me off like a slave?"

"Sheba, do you remember that kid goat you had when you were little?"

"Yes, but what does that have to do with me?"

"That goat was given to your family as part of a scheme called..." He paused unable to remember the name of the scheme.

"The Animal Bank?" I asked.

"Yes! That's it! The Animal Bank! Under the scheme, your father was to raise it until it was big enough to mate, have kids and..."

"Ah! I remember!" I interrupted. "We did mate it and after

it's milk finished we were to give one of the kids to another poor neighbor and keep the other to raise."

"So you remember! But do you remember what happened? You took the little kid as a pet and treated her like a little sister. And eventually..."

"Eventually I had to take my little pet to the butcher to be slaughtered. And my father took the money," I concluded angrily.

It was a painful memory. This incident had taken place the same year that my brother Matthew died. In my way, I had replaced little Matthew with a little kid. When I realized that my pet was destined for someone's mutton curry, I was furious. For many years I hated walking by a butcher's shop. I could only see my pet reflected in the eyes of the goat heads on display. Butchers display these heads in front of their shops like some kind of trophy.

I looked sternly at Pastor Stephen.

"Pastor, I don't want to be compared to the family goat, or a sacrificial lamb for that matter!"

He threw back his head and laughed. "Oh child, you are growing up! No, you are right. You are not a goat or lamb or any other beast. You are Sheba Victoria and you must live up to your name."

"Am I to be a queen then?" I teased, relieved at being able to speak so freely.

"Sheba, in India we believe that names are very important. You have been given two special names. Without God's help you cannot live up to either of them. Have you ever wondered why some people give their children such terrible-sounding names? When a baby is born to a family which has suffered some misfortune, they immediately give the child an odd name in order to divert 'Bad Luck's' attention. You have seen the black kajal dot on some baby's faces, put there to ward off the evil eye. The black dot may seem disfiguring to you but it is applied because these people believe that the evil spirit will not covet a blemished child."

"Hmmm..." I mused thinking of all the people I knew with weird names.

"Sheba, you have been given a name you can grow into. If you can overcome this situation, it will allow you to grow into your victory. And when you have won the victory, you will indeed be like a queen."

Pastor grinned at me, his teeth like pearls set in a warm, dark ocean. I was encouraged by his unwavering confidence in God and in me, an insignificant girl.

"Your father is under pressure too, Sheba. No matter what you think of him, he loves you and, though you do not understand it now, he truly wants the best for you. He wants you to have a good home, a good name, and money to feed and clothe yourself and your children. You are born into a society that places much importance on marriage for young women."

I tried to interrupt but Pastor held up a dark hand to silence me.

"Marriage is a safeguard, Sheba. Marriage keeps you with one man whose children will carry on his name. Through marriage you are sheltered, fed and clothed and you, in turn, will shelter, feed and clothe the next generation. 'Through the father is blood but through the mother is life and spirit'." He concluded with a reference to conventional Indian wisdom.

I wasn't sure I liked what I was hearing, but I let Pastor continue.

"I'm afraid, Sheba, that we don't know what to do with girls who have ideals and ambitions for their own lives apart from marriage. A girl who wants an education? This can be a risky venture for her parents. What if she fails to find a vocation? What if she can't support herself? Worse yet, she might remain unmarried and end up a misfit in society. Think of it Sheba, if girls wait too long to marry, they may end up too old to attract a good husband or have children! Then, what would people say of such a girl's father? They will say that he could not provide a decent groom for his daughter and he will become a failure in his own eyes and in the eyes of his community."

"But Pastor," I interrupted, determined to fight back, "if a girl should not receive an education why am I enrolled as a sponsored child? Why have the sponsorship program at all? Why help families educate their children and why do we..."

Pastor Stephen held up both hands in mock surrender.

153

"Sheba, I am all for your education and your future, for that matter. I am just reminding you of the kind of society you live in. When I was a child it was worse. If a girl was not married by the time she reached puberty it was considered a great sin on the part of her parents. Some religious teachers even said they would go to hell for such a thing. So keep in mind the kind of pressures we are dealing with here, and do not think these things will change over the span of a single generation or because of a single sponsorship program."

We fell silent. Outside, the usual din of traffic seemed to be fading away while the crickets began their metallic symphony.

"Have you filled your alabaster jar?"

I did not comprehend.

"In biblical times, people often kept their tears in a special jar. It was an alabaster jar of remembrance for suffering endured. It was said that no alabaster jar would ever become full because God would never allow us to suffer more than we could bear."

"I don't have a jar like that, Pastor," I replied meekly.

"No Sheba, and neither do I. But I still cry and believe that somewhere in heaven is a jar with our tears. And for every tear that we pour forth, our Lord sheds two."

"Then my jar must be nearly full by now!" I tried to laugh but tears seem to come out of nowhere to fill that cosmic jar of grief.

Pastor grew solemn and said quietly, "Sheba, what you did was your choice. I don't blame you for it but you alone will pay the consequences. When you swim against the stream you must be prepared for the rip tide."

"Am I a sinner for what I did?"

"I am not prepared to judge you on that account, Sheba. After all, we're all sinners.   Come! Let's get you home, your people are worried."

Pastor Stephen was about to extinguish the lantern when we heard a commotion on the stairs. I ran to see what it was about.

It was Mrs. Kalimuthu. Two of her grown children, a son and daughter, were helping her up the stairs. The two women were clinging to each other, as they would fall without the other's support. Her son Daniel was crying out for Pastor Stephen.

"Pastor Stephen, Pastor Stephen! Is Pastor in church?"

Daniel's cries brought Pastor Stephen springing to the top of the stairs. Twenty-four-year-old Daniel's father was a church elder and good friend of the pastor's.

Pastor Stephen grasped Daniel's hand and led the party into the hall. The women sobbed heartbreakingly and two small children nervously clung to Mrs. Kalimuthu's pallu. "What is it Daniel?" asked Pastor tensely.

Daniel looked long at his mother and blurted out desperately, "My father's been killed, Pastor!"

Pastor Stephen stiffened and then, putting an arm around Daniel's shoulders, he asked gently, "What happened?"

"He was cycling home with two fares in his rickshaw, an old lady and a young one. A lorry hit him from behind". Daniel sounded perplexed as though he couldn't understand how such a thing could happen.

"I told him not to be out after dark, he's got no lights on his rickshaw. How many times have I told him to stay off the roads when it's dark!" lamented the new widow.

I knew Mr. Kalimuthu's youngest son. He was in the same sponsorship program as me. His father had ridden a rickshaw along the streets of Perambur and Madras for years. On his earnings and with the aid from the sponsorship program, Mr. Kalimuthu and his wife had done the seemingly impossible by putting a son and a daughter through high school. They were still educating their youngest.

"What of the other two people?" the pastor quietly inquired.

"The lorry plowed into the rickshaw like a herd of angry buffaloes and pummeled them against a brick wall. They were all killed."

Pastor looked at me. It was clear he would have to stay with the family. Gently he told me to go home and said that he would try and drop by later that night. I wasn't looking forward to returning home without the pastor by my side but I knew that Mrs. Kalimuthu and her family needed him more than I that night.

It was after midnight when I reached home. My sins seemed to be piling up. I had willfully disobeyed my father by not meeting him at the church, I had stayed out till an unearthly hour, and I had walked home alone. Mr. Crenshaw, I couldn't plead insanity or ignorance in my defense. I only knew that I could not go through with this arranged marriage. And I could not flee my home - where would I go? I could only return and face the consequences of my stand.

I dreaded to think of what my father would do to me. The previous night I had bravely said 'He can't kill me, I'm his daughter' to Mrs. Venugopal. Now I wasn't so sure. He could always take me out of school and the sponsorship program. I would be forced to work at home making baskets or beedies. Wouldn't that be just as bad as being a child-bride in another family's house?

I put my hand on the door and gave it a gentle push. It swung open forcefully. Baskar stared at me from the other side of the threshold.

"Where have you been, Sheba? Everybody has been so worried about you!"

His dark eyes were worried but compassionate. I knew that whatever terror the night might hold, Baskar would be my side to support me.

Entering, I took in the situation with a glance. The three younger children were asleep under mosquito nets. Amma was huddled in a corner of the room. Beside her was my grandmother. They had obviously asked her to come and help them with this difficult situation. They didn't get up when they saw me. Their faces glistened with tears and I couldn't tell if they were tears of concern, humiliation or fear.

From the opposite corner came my father, striding towards me like a wild animal. I could see the rage in his eyes and at that moment I realized just how deeply I had humiliated my family.

"If you had no intention of meeting me at the church, why didn't you say so, girl?" He flung 'girl' at me as though it were an insult.

"I sat there stupidly for two hours, waiting for you, Sheba.

What could I say to Pandian and his mother? The story has already gotten around. What do I answer when people ask me 'Where is your daughter, Sunderraj?' ' Does she not know the time?' 'Has she forgotten the location of the church?' It was a stupid thing for you to humiliate me in this way!"

"Sheba, what's your reason for not doing as your father asked?" my mother wept.

Grandmother continued the onslaught. "Sheba, it is the way we live! You have no choice in the matter! If you don't get married you will be the lowest of women. You'll be an old spinster! Do you want that?"

I stood still, in the doorway, afraid to move. Baskar stood behind me, protective yet tense, aware that a storm could still erupt. I looked at my mother and grandmother. I wanted to say I was sorry for causing them so much trouble. I was sorry for bucking against tradition but I could not submit when my future and my dreams were at stake. I wanted so much to apologize but instead I blurted out, "I don't want to get married, I can't get married. Not now, not yet!"

"Sheba you are a mouth that I cannot support. You have failed me!"

"Appa..." I attempted a conciliatory response but before the words were out, a violent slap to my face sent me slamming against our small wooden table. A water bottle and tin cups went flying and landed noisily beside me on the floor. The disturbance woke up the sleeping children.

"Appa, what happened? Did you hurt, Sheba?" asked Sammy at once, and all three began to howl. It was a miserable scene.

Mr. Crenshaw I wish I didn't have to tell you about this very private and deplorable chapter of my life. However, as I said at the beginning of this letter, I must tell my story, all of it.

I registered the protests of my mother and grandmother mingling with the cries of my younger brothers and sister. What I felt, however, were the gentle arms of my brother as he attempted to shield me from further blows. Unfortunately for us both, Appa's rage was out-of-control. He flung Baskar aside, yanked me up, dragged me to the door and threw me on the ground outside.

"I don't want to see you in here again! You have done me no good. Your worst insult will be your last. Get out!"

And with that he delivered a harsh kick to my stomach that left me gasping for air, like a fish out of water. I was as much frightened by my breathlessness as I was at the prospects of a continued beating. But Baskar returned to my side like a gallant protector. Placing himself in the line of fire, as it were, he shouted, "What do you think you are doing? Sheba is your daughter; do you want to kill her? Kill me as well! Finish off your family if that's what you want!"

As Baskar yelled people began to stir in the neighboring huts. Many wandered out to see what the commotion was about but all stood at a safe distance and no one intervened. It was a family affair and up to us to resolve.

I was whimpering with fear and shame. And then, in the dark night I spotted two figures in white walking briskly towards us. Their faces were hidden by the dark and it was only when one figure smiled his trademark grin that I realized Pastor Stephen and his wife had come to my rescue.

Intuitively, Mrs. Stephen went to comfort the women of the household. Pastor Stephen unhesitatingly walked up to my father. His lips had a peculiar twist to them, as though part smile and part snarl. He put a hand on my father's shoulder and spoke quietly but earnestly. His presence exuded calm and I immediately sensed a change in the charged atmosphere.

I hope you aren't too shocked, Mr. Crenshaw. My father though an elder of the church is not a perfect man. Who is perfect? Were you to meet him, you would think him a lovely quiet man. And he is, for the most part. But he has a flash temper that is fearsome when aroused. Now, years later, I can understand what he must have been going through at the time. He was barely educated and had no hopes of rising any further in his profession. The constant strain of providing for a family of seven on an impossibly low income only fueled his frustrations. But it's only now, with the benefit of hindsight, that I can explain his behavior. As a child, I only wondered at his lack of love and concern for one of his own children.

Pastor spoke to Appa for about five minutes. Baskar crouched beside me as I sobbed. Then Pastor Stephen called us all into the house. We had been scattered like a small flock of frightened sheep. Appa seemed to have undergone a complete change of heart. As I said, he has a flash temper, diffused as quickly as it is ignited. Poor Appa could not look any of us in the eye. Pastor had his arm around Appa in manly consolation while his wife stood close to Amma and my grandmother. The younger children clung to Amma's sari. Baskar and I sat shoulder to shoulder in the doorway.

Pastor began to speak softly. I could tell at once that he was going to deliver a message. He began.

"A Sanskrit proverb says, 'Though you wash charcoal a thousand times, yet the blackness will not come out', but I don't agree. I have seen charcoal turn white when it is kept in the fire for a long time. The Sunderraj family is passing through a fire. It is called the furnace of life and in that furnace we all get burned. Sheba, you are being made white and pure by the testing of this fire. You do not know it now, but years from now, you will thank your father for qualities developed in you that are not seen this night."

Pastor looked at me unsmilingly and I felt smaller than a speck of dust. I couldn't stop crying. I cried out of anger and grief and sadness. I could hear sobbing from around me. We were a tightly knit family and had never known such a violent ripping of the fabric of our lives.

"You cry now Sheba, but some day you will weep tears of thankfulness for your father and mother and brother and sisters."

And then Pastor Stephen raised his hands heavenwards and looked up at the dark rafters. His eyes seemed to see something beyond the roof.

"Sthothiram, sthothiram," he shouted which means 'hallelujah' in Tamil, Mr. Crenshaw. Pastor's words gained momentum until he was like a locomotive rushing down the tracks.

"You have so many things to be thankful for. I remember the time I first set eyes on Grandmother Thangamal and her four beautiful granddaughters at the Perambur train station. At once I saw that you had the complexion of outcasts, Anglo-Indians, who did not feel at home either in India or England. You were casteless and did not have a place in the society you were born into. You looked forlorn and your eyes did not possess the sparkle of joy that I am now accustomed to seeing in this beautiful family, sthothiram!

"I saw you as the Lord saw Israel in its infancy. Your family was like a tiny child without hope. And then I heard the Lord telling me to approach you and say one word. As I stood in front of you, you looked up, expecting me to ask for a plate of the iddly you were selling. Your eyes were vacant; you expected nothing out of the ordinary. I spoke one word: 'Live', oh sthothiram!"

We listened attentively to the Pastor's storytelling. I noticed that Mrs. Stephen was gently rocking her rotund body back and forth, hands supinely raised to the powerful cadence of her husband's sermon.

"Live, I said to each of you and you looked at me and received the Lord's miracle and blessing of life. You began to attend our church and you blossomed like wild jasmine. And as Victoria began to grow in grace, Mohan saw her purity and desired her for his wife, sthothiram!

"On your wedding day you were clothed in fine linen, the finest that had ever adorned your body. Your grandmother Thangamal bestowed precious jewels on you; trinkets given to her by your grandfather who deserted your family and returned to England.

"You were blessed within the first year of marriage with a daughter. I know Mohan was disappointed for he had foolishly wagered on having a son. Yet, Mohan, you carried your baby daughter high above the waters saving her from the wrath of the storm.

"God has proven his faithfulness to you in many other ways. You had enemies who were determined to destroy your family. A shaman was employed to separate Victoria and Mohan. Victoria's sickness was nearly unto death but God thwarted the plans of the evil one. In a dream, God revealed to me cursed objects buried under the very threshold of your house. An enemy of yours had retrieved strands of Mohan's hair from the barber and mingled it with the bones of wild animals. This was buried secretly in front of your house and, while you slept, a curse was called down upon your family. But God is not fooled, God is not mocked, sthothiram, sthothiram, sthothiram! We dug up the curse and flung the evil back from where it came!

"When little Matthew was taken, from you were comforted with the knowledge that he was safe in the arms of Jesus. And even in these economically tough times, have you ever gone a day without food? No! God's hand has been upon this family. You may live in a slum but remember; in God's eyes you are princes and princesses. We have come this far and we will continue until we have arrived in the land of glory with all God's children!"

Pastor Stephen didn't stop there. He continued to preach for quite a while. The adults silently wiped away a few tears; we children slumped with exhaustion.

Mr. Crenshaw, I wish I could tell you that Pastor Stephen's sermon brought about an immediate reconciliation within our family. But it didn't happen quite that way. His sermon diffused the crisis and we all lay down together in our usual row. I suspect, however, that Appa wished he had another place to go that night. The flames of raw emotion had been put out but the embers still glowed in our hearts.

Having crossed the river yourself,

Get others across

Sanskrit Proverb

ℒ 21 ℒ

For the next two weeks, Appa said very little to either Baskar or myself. There was a pall of gloom over our household made worse by Appa's brooding. Nothing more was said about my marriage.

As far as I was concerned, I had done what I had done in my best interests. Now, having fought for my right to a better future I had to figure out a way to secure it.

First, I would have to be even more diligent in my studies in order to get good marks in my upcoming final exams. I was determined to show my father that I was a capable student. Second, I was determined to help Chopu pass the exams too. The next four weeks were crucial if we were to make it happen. I wasn't crossing this river without Chopu.

I've just realized, Mr. Crenshaw, that I haven't gotten around to telling you what happened with Javid. The last time he entered my story was when my teacher discovered his love poems written to me on the back of my geography maps. Well, let's go back to what happened after that.

The morning after the parent-teacher meeting, I found Javid waiting for me at the bus stop. I hadn't seen him after he'd handed me my maps and he must have been surprised that his poems hadn't evoked any response from me. Little did he know that I hadn't seen them till that dreadful meeting with Amma and Mrs. Manikam.

The sight of him made me angry and I stared impassively at his face. Javid looked back defiantly. His usual playful smile was missing.

"Today you make the choice, Sheba. Tell me yes or no."

I sighed at this familiar question. I was about to answer when he dangled a small dark brown bottle in front of my face.

"Answer me now, Sheba Victoria. Say that you will love me more than as a friend and I will throw this away. Continue to deny me your love and I will drink this bottle of poison."

I don't know what he expected to hear but I'm sure it wasn't, "Oh, go away, Javid!"

He looked stunned. I was completely sick of his behavior. He had tried my patience to the limit and I had neither the will nor the emotional strength to put up with his foolish games.

His voice was hysterically high-pitched. "Okay, I'll go away if you insist, Sheba. I'll drink this poison. But you must know that I have written a letter, Sheba. It is a very clever letter, with poetry and prose. The letter is addressed to the police and I have told them you are to blame for my death. You will go to prison for my death."

"Javid," I snapped, "throw away your bottle. And for God's sake, grow up!"

"You can't put me off forever," he countered shakily.

"How can you live with yourself, Javid?" I shot back. "Do you think you can bully me or anyone into loving you? What kind of love would that be?"

I had called his bluff. To this day, I don't know if that bottle really contained poison or not. Javid looked at me indignantly as if he couldn't believe that I would be so hard-hearted.

My bus arrived and I jumped into it. It would be months before I saw Javid again.

Chopu and I quickly got our joint study sessions underway. We met in the evenings at my house. I became aware of many other students who desperately needed tutoring but couldn't afford the high cost of tuition. When word got out that I was assisting Chopu with English and that Chopu was giving me math instruction, other students asked if they could join our study group. But the group soon outgrew our tiny house so one evening I visited Pastor Stephen at his church to make an unusual request.

As I entered his study, I saw that he was with Valar, his son, who had been appointed Sponsorship Program Director.

"Pastor Stephen, is it possible to open the church for a study hour in the evenings?" I came straight to the point.

"You want to have an evening Bible study hour, Sheba? Very good! I will ask Elder Prabakaran if he can..."

"No, no Appa! The children want to use the church as a study place. For schoolwork," clarified Valar who wisely understood the nature of my request.

"You do not want to study the Bible?" asked Pastor, a little disappointed.

"It's not like that, Pastor. We will continue to do that on Sundays evenings," I hastily assured him. "But, there are some students who find it difficult to study in their homes. Kerosene is costly and so some parents do not allow their children to use the kerosene lamps for a long time. Some homes are just too noisy. We want to know if we can study here, with the electric lights on. I will be responsible!" I ventured.

"But, Sheba, if you come here, how will I pay for the electricity bill? We can scarcely afford to turn on the lights as it is."

"Appa, let's open the church to the children. You can always suggest that they bring their families for the Sunday worship service."

Pastor's eyes brightened at his son's suggestion. Here was a way to increase his flock and, perhaps, bring in a few extra rupees that would go towards the electricity bill. Valar had inherited his father's qualities of kindness and generosity but was also blessed with an extra dose of savvy.

"So, Sheba," Valar continued, "You are welcome to bring this study group of yours. When will you start?"

"Mr. Valar, I would like to start tomorrow if possible."

"What shall I write on the notice board? Who shall I say is meeting?"

His question had me stumped. Who were we? I simply thought of us as a study group but if Valar wrote 'study group', we would surely be interrupted by people who had come thinking a Bible study group was going on.

"We are the tutors," I decided finally.

"Hmmm, should we use the word 'tutors'? People may think you're charging a tuition fee." Valar looked at me with mock suspicion, "You aren't charging a tuition fee, are you?"

"No. No!" I replied indignantly. "We are simply peers helping one another."

"Ah! So let's call you the 'Peer Tutors'," he said with a satisfied smile.

Pastor Stephen, with a typical Indian love for acronyms, shouted joyously, "P.T.! P.T.! You are the P.T.s.!"

Valar accompanied me down the stairs. "Sheba," he said quietly, "this is a golden opportunity! Do you know how many students commit suicide at exam time each year? Hundreds! It is especially bad among tenth standard students whose families pin all their hopes on success. The possibility of a failure is so fearful that death seems the only option for many children."

I shuddered at the recollection of a school acquaintance that ate insecticide after her teacher ridiculed her for failing a test. Fortunately, she survived but I knew of many others who had ended their lives rather than live in shame or cause potential hardship for their families.

"You're doing a good thing, Sheba. How many attend your PT group?"

"Seven. We would like to continue even during the exam week." I was a little nervous at speaking to Valar as though I were an adult but his confidence in me and his willingness to listen and, it appeared, learn from me gave me a new sense of confidence.

Our peer tutor group began with little fanfare. We began the next evening and decided to meet six days a week. Each evening was assigned a subject. We had to cover English, Math, Geography, History, Science, and Language, which was either Tamil or Hindi. Students gifted in a subject assisted those who needed help. Our PT group soon grew to twenty-two.

Our study sessions at the church provided a place of security and serenity for children who rarely found either at their homes in the slums. A place to study in peace, good lighting in the evening, and students who were willing and able to assist their peers were the keys to our success.

And that, Mr. Crenshaw, is how our model for assisted learning began. The Peer Tutors has become an ongoing program that we employ in both our area sponsorship program and at the school where I teach. It has been very effective among children who are too poor to pay for special tuition.

Our PT group was an informal gathering, but word got out about it. Two teachers from a local school were outright indignant. They showed up at the church one evening. Fortunately Valar was there. Though obviously not our peer, he had offered to tutor and was a great favorite among the group.

That evening we were studying English. When the two teachers appeared at the top of the stairs, we were sitting in small groups, quietly going over our English material. Mistaking them for parents, Valar said politely, "Welcome sirs, can I be of assistance?"

Both the teachers also took after-class tuition. A couple of their former students were part of our PT group. One of the teachers, Mr. Gnanaraj, brushed aside Valar's civilities and loudly asked, "Why are you all interfering with the teacher's profession?"

Mr. Gnanaraj was very wide and short. Thin wisps of straight, black-dyed hair shot upwards on his head while his bulging eyes surveyed the students.

"I am seeing very well what is going on here young man. You are meddling where you have no business in the trade of a teacher. I have a half-mind to call the police as most assuredly you are teaching without a license!"

"Sir," Valar meekly replied, "we may be interfering with the teacher's tradition but I can assure you no one is teaching here. These students are simply studying for exams. I should think you would be pleased with their diligence."

Valar had struck a nerve when he used the word 'tradition'. Many of our teachers demanded forty rupees each month for special tuition. Students who didn't go for tuition were unfairly penalized in class in the hope that their parents would send them for tuition.

Valar managed to get rid of the pesky duo. The next person to comment on our PT group was the headmaster of my school. He visited the evening tutorial and expressed whole-hearted satisfaction at our enthusiasm and determination to do well in the exams. His support effectively silenced our critics.

As the exams drew near, Chopu and I dared to feel that we would get through them. The examinations papers, Mr. Crenshaw, are prepared by a central body and sent to schools all over the State so that entire tenth standard student body simultaneously sits for the same exam.

Dear Mr. Crenshaw, our last evening of PT was an exciting one. Most of the students felt a confidence they would not have otherwise known. After the session, Valar congratulated us and asked if he could pray for each of us. His warmth and belief in us gave us extra strength. Failure was far from our minds when we said our farewells that night.

After the session, Chopu and I walked to the well together. Even though she had a distance to go, we couldn't resist a visit to our old haunt. We both reveled in our renewed friendship and as we stood by the well we reminisced about our happy childhood years.

"Do you remember our twin sisters?" I asked hopefully.

"Of course, Sheba! Do you remember what we wished for?"

"Well, you wanted to marry the Chief Collector!"

"Yes, and you said you would marry for love. Do remember that?"

"No," I said telling a barefaced lie, "I don't remember that."

I felt ashamed at my lie and asked God to forgive me. I hadn't yet told Chopu of my disastrous arranged marriage experience. I had pushed it to the back of my mind while I concentrated on my studies.

I changed the subject. "What will you do Chopu? After the exams are over?"

"I don't know. It depends. If I do well then I'm going to study computer science with the grant. If I fail, well..." Chopu made a comical gesture by grabbing her throat with her right hand and sticking out her tongue in a mock hanging. But it wasn't funny and I knew she was under incredible pressure.

We leaned against the well and watched a full moon appear from behind the clouds and shine above the ragged skyline of the Maduma Nagar slums. I held Chopu's hand and prayed.

I committed our relationship, the coming exams, and all the students taking them, to God. I prayed for peace upon Chopu knowing that she had done all she could in her preparation. I prayed that she would trust in her God-given memory and do well.

"Meet me here after the exams. We'll compare notes!" With that she hugged me and we parted, our moon-cast shadows flowing after us down the dark footpaths.

'Man's children are his fortune,' say the wise,

From each one's deeds his varied fortunes rise.

The Kurral

When I returned home, only Baskar was awake. A kerosene lamp flickered dimly, casting its feeble light on his faded paperback textbook. I tiptoed in and stood still, listening for a moment to the distinctive sounds of slumber made by each member of my family. Appa lay on his back and snored rhythmically. He sounded like an electric saw. Amma, Kalyani, and Jayakumar breathed silently. Sammy emitted little squeals of excitement, no doubt caught up in an adventurous dream.

How much longer would I live in this house? Where would life take us and what would our individual destinies be? In my weariness, I wanted only to sprawl out on my mat and sleep but I knew I had to review math and history before going to bed. I joined Baskar on his mat. His lips moved silently as he mouthed his lessons. He paused to smile at me, his eyes crinkling with love. I smiled back and opened my books.

Baskar had always been a good student and his steady progress was sure to clinch him a scholarship. I was, I confess, a little erratic, shining in subjects I loved and scraping through in subjects I dreaded. Baskar had brains while I had ... at that moment I wasn't exactly sure what I had, Mr. Crenshaw.

I'm nearing the end of this journal of my sponsored years, Mr. Crenshaw, and I wish I could say with assurance exactly what my defining quality is in life. As I said in the beginning, I am a listener and storyteller. Baskar has been blessed with an aptitude for learning while I have been blessed with an aptitude for wonder. I find myself continually marveling at life, its incredible twists and turns, its inconsistencies and its sheer beauty. I am aware that we are mortal and that each day counts more than we think.

The first time I became aware of my own mortality was that night as I sat studying beside Baskar. I looked up for a moment at Baskar's face, intense with concentration. I looked at my family, asleep and free from everyday cares. That moment caused my heart to worship, to acknowledge God's undeniable presence in my life. And in that hot, miserable hovel I knew true peace and the joy of living.

It was about one o'clock in the morning when I finally went to sleep. My mind drifted...

I was at the well. The moon was high and incredibly bright, as though it had overdosed on the sun's rays. From below, I heard the sound of childish laughter, the giggles rippled upwards. I was startled. Carefully leaning over the wall I whispered, "Who is there?"

"Sheba, have you forgotten your sisters in the well?" came the reply.

"I haven't forgotten you. I think of you every time I visit the well."

The two sisters in the well giggled once more.

"Should we tell her?" whispered one.

"No," said the other, "she'll find out soon enough."

Through their giggling, I could hear Chopu's cackle. I became confused and climbed on top of the well wall. Looking down, I shouted, "Tell me what? What did you do with Chopu? Tell me or I will jump into the well and make you tell me, you naughty twins."

But the twins sank deeper below the water, smiling and waving till I couldn't see them anymore. The sound of clapping and the clanging of washtubs startled me. Mrs. Jyothimani was coming towards me, agitatedly flapping her free hand.

"Get away from the well, you dirty bird, you'll soil my laundry!" she shouted. I became a crow and flew straight towards the moon that became as bright as the sun. I looked down and saw myself walking with my family down a dirt lane in Maduma Nagar. It was a warm, cheery morning, the kind that comes after a night of rain, when everything, even our slum, felt and looked sparklingly clean. Our family was walking together as we did on the day of Valar's wedding. Appa and Amma brought up the rear. They were smiling and talking to one another while we children walked in front. Sammy ran ahead, playing football with a stone. Kalyani and I held hands. We had flowers in our hair and our clothes were clean and smelled of laundry detergent. Baskar and Jayakumar were animatedly discussing cricket.

We arrived not at a wedding as I'd expected, but at an airport. It was situated on the big playground at school. A gleaming silver airplane was parked at one side. A few people stood around, and at the top of the stairs leading to the door of the plane was Javid. He was dressed in a white shirt with a red tie and white trousers with a black belt. We were at the airport to see him off because he was going to visit his mother in Saudi Arabia. I had never seen Javid so happy. He often played the joker to hide his hurt, but now he was truly happy. After he waved to everyone, he went inside. The plane's motors got very loud and the plane raced down the runway and rose into the bright sky. It flew high and we all watched as it went straight into the sun. The sun was so bright it hurt my eyes.

"Wake up, Sheba! We have to fetch the water! I opened my eyes with a start. Appa stood above me, shining a flashlight straight in my eyes. It was five in the morning. My head hurt from lack of sleep.

"Appa, can't we do this tomorrow morning? My first exam is today and I need more sleep," I groaned.

"No child, tomorrow I have to leave home early. I am taking a batch of seat cushions from the factory to the city. Today is our turn to collect water. Come let's go," he answered firmly but patiently.

I groggily set about collecting buckets. This early morning water collection ritual was a chore I'd always shared with my father. Our community of nearly 2000 people had one well. We were allotted days on which we could collect water for cooking and drinking.

This water had to last us two days till our turn came again. Amma, who had been weakened by a bout of tuberculosis when she was young, couldn't carry the heavy buckets. As the eldest, it had always been my responsibility to aid Appa in this task.

Appa had actually allowed me an extra two hours of sleep. Normally we were up by three in the morning on water collection days.

Appa and I swung into routine once we reached the well. One of us pumped, while the other hefted the bucket home, careful not to spill a drop. It was a feat of balance. As I pumped water into the last of our seven buckets, Appa asked casually, "Do you feel well-prepared for your exams, Sheba?"

"I think so, Appa. Our study times at the church have helped, even Chopu is feeling more confident now."

My father nodded as though deep in thought. He was not a man to reveal what was going on in his mind.

"Sheba," he said before lifting the bucket, "God is with you, child. You will succeed."

Appa spoke quietly but those few words were the most significant ones he had ever said to me. Till that moment I had never really believed in myself. I had never been absolutely sure that my struggle for a better future was worthwhile. Appa's words dispelled all my self-doubt. He believed in me and from that moment, I believed in myself.

March 3, 1986

Dear Sheba,

Greetings to you, dear one.

Sheba, it is with great joy that I write this letter as it marks eight years since we began to sponsor you. I must admit, when we started we had no idea what we were getting into. We thought we would send a monthly contribution and be satisfied with the pleasure of knowing that we were helping an unknown little girl in faraway India.

But that has not been the case, Sheba. You are not an unknown little girl. We feel as though we truly know you. We have prayed for you almost daily (and I regret the days we missed, Sheba, but I confess we are only human), your picture has always been up on our refrigerator, and over the past eight years we have tracked your progress through school, church, and your community.

I can only hope and pray that you have been blessed with hope through your sponsorship and that our heavenly father will open many doors of opportunity for you.

I turn 68 this month. You've just begun to run your race; I'm getting close to the finish line. I like to think that Auntie Sue Ellen and I are passing the torch to you, Sheba, and that you will run with patience the good race set before you.

Sheba, I cannot hide the fact that Auntie Sue Ellen is getting weaker by the day and her future is very uncertain. We are grateful that Randy and his wife Cindy live nearby. They have taken over the farm and I assist my son in the chores I once taught him to do. At least, Auntie and I are able to remain on our farm and not be carted off to one of those assisted living homes where they put old folks out to pasture.

One final thing, dear. One. I have done a little investigating and contacted the good folk who work with your sponsorship program there. I asked if it were possible to help you during the next stage of your education. Our intention was to provide some modest support. When we found out how much your two-year pre-college course and your three-year college tuition would cost, we decided that we would like to provide the funds for the next five years of your education. The money we send will cover tuition, books, materials and travel. I trust you will be able to attend a school or college near your community and continue to live at home. Please let us know if this is fine with you, as we do not wish to presume on your personal goals.

I am looking at a picture that I keep here, on my writing desk. It is of a little girl in a school uniform. She looks shy, yet there is a determination in her face that tells me she can do anything she sets her sharp mind to (and yes, I am smiling as I write this). The little girl is you, Sheba Victoria. You were once a girl of promise; you are now a woman of destiny. Never forget where you came from. Never forget where you are going.

With love (and appreciation),

Clay and Auntie Sue Ellen Crenshaw

By the time Appa and I returned from the well, the sun was up. It was a hot, muggy morning, typical of early March. I bolted down two chappathis dipped in vegetable sambar. I checked to see if I had taken my exam board, pens, pencils, ruler, and eraser. Suitably armed, I set off for school.

In the bus, I prayed for Chopu and myself and all the others in our PT group. I couldn't help but feel sad that Javid wouldn't be taking the exam with us. We had all grown up together and in spite of his silly infatuation for me, I regarded him as a friend for whom I wished nothing but the best.

Javid's fatal flaw was his inability to work hard for what he wanted. He clowned around and expected easy results. As school-work became tougher, Javid began to slacken. Chopu and he attended the same school and she said that he simply stopped trying. He hardly attended class. We felt sorry for him because we knew he was ambitious and wanted a better life, but his refusal to work towards it disappointed us. Chopu told him about the PT group but he laughed it off and refused to attend.

The next week went by in a blur of question papers, answer sheets, pens flying, clocks ticking, late night cramming, early morning revision ... like every student before and after me, I wondered if I would survive the experience.

"Stop writing!" came the command.

Hundreds of pens obediently clattered to their desks. The answer sheets were collected.

"You may leave," said the teacher.

Hundreds of students poured out of the examination hall whooping with delight. The exams were over. A week of tension found vent in excited chattering and cheering. Just knowing that I didn't have to rush home and study for another exam made me want to shout for joy. I collected my belongings and headed for the exit.

"Just a minute, Sheba," called Mr. Shankar. I skidded to a halt and looked back at him impatiently.

"I want to discuss something with you," he explained.

Trying to disguise my impatience to be out of that dreaded

hall, I walked to his table and stood before him.

"Well? How did you do the exams?"

"Mr. Shankar, I must wait for the results to know that!"

He grinned. "You must have some idea."

And then I couldn't hide my joy anymore. "I think I did well, Mr. Shankar."

"You have been a good student, Sheba. What are your future plans?"

"I'm going to complete two more years of school and then I'm going to college," I told him and, Mr. Crenshaw, I almost burst with pride when I said the word 'college'.

"College?" Mr. Shankar's eyes widened.

"Yes!" I said happily, "my sponsor in America has offered to pay for everything I will need in the next five years of my studies. The letter came two days ago."

Mr. Shankar reached over the table and grabbed my hand. Shaking it hard, he beamed and said, "Congratulations Sheba! Congratulations!"

"Thank you, sir, thank you!" I replied thrilled that someone as respected as Mr. Shankar shared my joy.

"Sheba," he went on, "I was impressed with the results of your study group, the Peer Tutors. The idea appeals to me. Some of the other teachers and the headmaster have been discussing the merits of this program and would like to talk to you about starting more such groups. If more students had this sort of support, I am certain there would be fewer failures."

I could hardly believe my ears. I couldn't imagine myself lecturing the teachers and the headmaster on how to run Peer Tutor groups.

"Let's talk next week. I'll send word to you and we can fix a meeting."

"Okay sir, bye sir!" I replied and ran out of the hall. I desperately wanted to meet Chopu and I was certain I knew where to find her.

I jumped off the bus and began to run. I passed the public latrines and Mr. Jagan's kiosk. I heard him ask why I was in hurry but I couldn't stop to reply. I sped past Mr. Venugopal's house and the sleeping dogs. I burst around the corner of his lane and pulled up short. I had expected to see a lone figure leaning against the well wall. Instead I could see the backs of at least fifty people making enough noise for a hundred.

I fought my way through the crowd. I could hear Mrs. Jyothimani complaining, "Why these children love to play near the well, I don't know. I am always chasing them off!"

I could hear Mr. Babu call urgently, "Somebody get more rope! We need more rope!"

"Call the fire brigade!" said another.

I reached the front and stared blankly at the well.

"Oh Chopu! No!" I thought. My heart stood still. Nothing mattered at that moment - my marks, the bright future that stretched ahead of me - nothing mattered if Chopu wasn't going to be there to share in the blessing. Tears began to roll down my face. If only I'd arrived earlier, I berated myself. Why had Mr. Shankar delayed me for so long?

"Tie one end around the trunk of that tree," ordered Mr. Babu and some men ran to obey. "Watch out for the ends, it's badly frayed."

Several men took up positions along the rope, ready to pull when ordered.

Mr. Babu lowered himself by the rope into the depths of the well. I wanted to close my eyes and run away. How could this have happened? Had the extra tutoring come too late?

"Did someone jump into the well?"

The voice startled me and I jumped, not just because I was startled but, also, because the voice belonged to Chopu.

I hugged her hard. "I thought you were in the well!" I cried.

"What would I be doing in the well?" she asked with a puzzled frown.

At that moment, a muffled voice came from within the well.

"Yes, I've tied the rope around my waist. Start pulling."

Mr. Babu emerged from the well, wet and grinning broadly.

He untied the rope from his waist and threw it back down while fielding the many questions of the curious onlookers. "Stand back, stand back. No, I don't know why he's sitting in the well. Ask him yourself once he comes up. Tied it around your waist? Good. Now pull!"

The men began to heave with all their might. Mr. Sanjeev grabbed a bucket of water and began to pour some on the hemp rope to prevent it from fraying as it dragged against the cement parapet wall.

"Hey!" yelled an irate voice. "Who's pouring water on me? I'm half-drowned as it is!"

Chopu and I looked at each other in astonishment.

"It's Javid!" we shouted in unison.

Javid emerged at the top of the well and eager hands heaved him over the side to safety. He looked more humiliated than battered and scowled ungratefully at his rescuers. It looked as if his leg was broken or his ankle sprained. His rescuers scooped him up and rushed off towards the Perambur-Madras Highway.

"Taking him to Dr. Nagpal's clinic!" called someone.

"I hope they have enough money," I thought.

The crowd split up into small groups, each eagerly recounting the events of the afternoon, the roles they played in the rescue and speculating on how and why Javid had been found in the well.

As we turned to leave, Chopu turned to me with her characteristic cheeky grin and said, "I wonder if Javid was visiting the twins down there?"

We both laughed till our sides ached. It was just what we needed to let go of all the tension we'd suffered that past week.

When we sobered up I asked Chopu how she'd fared in her exams.

"First tell me how you did," she insisted.

"I did fine," I said, trying to downplay the fact that I knew I'd done extremely well.

Chopu looked at my face and smiled.

"Well then," she said happily, "we both did fine."

December 13, 1986

Dear Sheba,

I regret to say that Auntie Sue Ellen passed away this morning. There are no words to express my loss and sorrow. This is short as there are many preparations for her funeral and I cannot write much. Please know that Auntie loved and prayed for you as one of her own.

'Behold, I show you a mystery; we shall not all sleep, but we shall all be changed.

In a moment, in the twinkling of an eye, at the last trump: for the trumpet shall sound, and the dead shall be raised incorruptible, and we shall be changed.' 1 Corinthians 15:51-52

Sheba, it only remains now for us to be changed. May God bless and prosper your future.

Clay Crenshaw

I've almost finished my letter, Mr. Crenshaw. But before I forget, let me tell you how Javid found himself at the bottom of the well.

After months of frittering away his time and laughing at friends who were studying, he suddenly did a complete about-turn. On the first day of the exams, Javid appeared in class. But as he entered the classroom, the teacher in-charge spotted him and actually gave a hoot of laughter.

"You!" he said scornfully. "What are you planning to do here? Students who have earned their right to take the exams are welcome here. You, Javid, have done nothing but mock the education system."

Javid was about to make one of his famous retorts but was disconcerted when his classmates erupted into laughter at the teacher's words. He turned and fled in shame.

For the rest of the week, Javid slunk around outside the school watching his peers steeped in exam fever. On the last day of the exams, as he watched his jubilant classmates stream out of the exam hall cheering and celebrating, something in him snapped.

He ran straight to the well and jumped up on the wall. I suspect, Mr. Crenshaw, that the melodrama of the situation appealed to him. I doubt he meant to jump in. But someone who saw a figure balancing on the well wall gave a shout. Javid turned around to look, lost his balance and plummeted into the well.

Fortunately for Javid, our water table drops considerably in the hot season. He hit the water and landed on the squelchy well bottom. He straightened up automatically and was surprised to find himself standing only neck-deep in water. The next visitor to the well was Mrs. Jyothimani who lowered her bucket at top speed straight on to Javid's head. His anguished cries caused her to peer into the well.

"What ever are you doing in the well, young man?" she bellowed.

You know the rest.

But the story has a happy ending, Mr. Crenshaw. Javid wisely decided to go back to school the next academic year. He finished his tenth standard, passed the exams and began to work with his uncle who had set up a computer repair shop. I see him once in a while. He greets me shiftily, looks down, and rushes off.

Dear Mr. Crenshaw, you are now up-to-date with my childhood. As I said at the beginning of this letter, I have written things that I could never have written as a child. I hope I've given you a deeper understanding of what life was like for a sponsored girl growing up in India, and what your sponsorship meant to me. I am not sure I wrote this letter purely for your benefit, Mr. Crenshaw, for it has been a journey that I've had to embark upon as well.

My mother is still alive. She lives in the same house and stills weaves baskets in the afternoons. Appa died three years ago from cerebral malaria. I felt the loss deeply because Appa and I developed a true, strong and understanding relationship only after I started college. But I'm grateful to God for the years I enjoyed Appa, not just as a father but, also, as a friend and ally. Though he would never have been able to tell you himself, he was very grateful to you for sponsoring my education.

To my lasting joy, Appa lived to see me married. I had an arranged marriage, Mr. Crenshaw. Well, I say 'arranged' but I must confess that in a way, Deena and I arranged for our parents to arrange our marriage. There was a small amount of what Chopu might call legerdemain. So you see, in the end, I did marry for love. But that's another story, Mr. Crenshaw, and I doubt you'd have the patience to read through another ten-year account of my life.

Baskar went to college and then attended a Bible seminary. He now pastors a small church in Bihar. It nearly broke our hearts to see him leave. My gentle and brave brother works tirelessly to improve the lives of the dalits, the outcasts of Indian society. We couldn't be more proud of him.

Sammy still tells stories but uses a computer to do so. He writes for the Tamil Nadu Journal of Youth. At present, he's researching a story on the famous outlaws of South India.

And what of Chopu? My dear vivacious friend studied hard and went on to become a flight attendant with Air India. She gets to see the world and adventures still seem to follow her wherever she goes. But I'm a little worried about her, Mr. Crenshaw. She's twenty-nine and still unmarried!

God bless you, Mr. Crenshaw. I hope you'll agree that I have indeed turned out well in the end.

And yes, I am smiling as I write this.

Sheba Victoria

Chennai
June 16, 1999